D1629802

LEVERHULME'S RIVINGTON

(The story of the Rivington 'Bungalow')

M D Smith

Printed and Published by Nelson Brothers Printers Ltd.,
Fellery Street, Chorley, Lancs.

ISBN 0 9508772 1 2 (Hardback)

1st published March 1984
1st Reprint September 1984

"Ruins Yet Beauteous in Decay"
(Robert Burns 1756 – 1796)

Dedicated to the memory of
William Mason
(14.9.1906 – 9.3.1983)

View of the front of 'The Bungalow' from the main driveway. Note the dovecote and second storey which date it after the ballroom was built. Stones on the left were for the construction of a rockery about 1930.

Acknowledgements

I wish to thank all those who have assisted me in any way whatsoever in the compilation of this work and without wishing to detract from the efforts of those not specifically mentioned I owe especial thanks to the following:–

My wife Andrea and her brother Paul Barry Mason without whose help, and encouragement I doubt the work would ever have been completed.

MISS J. M. ALDERSLEY – North Road, Ambleside, Cumbria (Cover)
FRED ASHWORTH – Pall Mall Cottages, Rivington.
AILSA BOWERS – Port Sunlight Information Centre.
MARTIN BROWNLOW – Brownlow Road, Horwich.
KEVIN CAMPBELL – Bolton Library Archivist.
MRS. CORNTHWAITE – Higher Kit Brow Ellel, Galgate.
ANTHONY CUBBERLEY – Oak Lane, Sevenoaks, Kent.
MRS. DOROTHY DARBYSHIRE – Babylon Lane, Heath Charnock.
HAROLD DICKINSON – Lever Park Avenue, Horwich.
GEOFFREY FAIRBROTHER – Crown Lane, Horwich.
MRS. PHYLLIS HAWORTH – Woodland Drive, Warton, Nr. Preston
MR. & MRS. G. KAY – Victoria Road, Horwich.
MISS DOROTHY KERSHAW – Major Bottoms, Anderton.
MR. JACK KINGS – Ainslie Road, Horwich.
MRS. IDA MASON, Babylon Lane, Anderton.
MRS. VIOLET PENDLEBURY – Ladycrosse Drive, Whittle-le-Woods.
MRS. G. M. SARGENT – Fifth Avenue, Bolton
BRIAN SMITH – Journal Offices, Horwich.
JOHN SMITH – Harts Houses, Horwich.
KEITH SHONE – Westgate Avenue, Bolton.

The Publishers will be pleased to receive any information,
particularly photographs, which complement this work.

Contents

Rivington Village Green and Post Office from Sheep House Lane. (Circa 1905).

Foreword

The picturesque village of Rivington remains virtually unspoiled despite being situated in Lancashire's industrial heartland. The expansion of trade in the mid nineteenth century, particularly from the Port of Liverpool, seems to have contributed, indirectly, to this circumstance. Increase in the population of the city, plus new awakening in awareness of sanitation and cleanliness, resulted in the Corporation of Liverpool looking for a source of pure, clean water for its residents. The wells used in the City were less than hygienic and there was a high incidence of cholera and typhoid.

The water catchment area on the moors above Rivington was harnessed to feed a series of Reservoirs which were constructed in the Valley below. The original supply of water was coloured brown and tainted but these initial shortcomings soon disappeared and the supply became reputed for its clarity and purity. Thenceforward Liverpool Corporation have carefully monitored the number and type of buildings which were constructed on its holdings with the specific purpose of preventing pollution of the water supply, and have thus preserved the area from the attention of the industrialist and property developer.

Over the years, since the construction of the reservoirs, nature has mellowed and camouflaged the effect of man's hand and the "Rivington Lakes" form part of the enchanting beauty of this place. On the barren slopes of the moorland, rising above the reservoirs, there once existed a palatial residence surrounded by landscaped garden areas of breathtaking beauty.

Traces of the, once magnificent "Bungalow" can still be seen and there is ample evidence of the scale of the grounds in the tumbledown remains of summer houses and stone pathways. There is a sadness about the place for me, as when something beautiful is lost for ever, and my purpose in writing this book is an attempt to recreate a realistic impression of how the "Bungalow" looked in its hey-day.

The Bungalow, Rivington, Lancashire, was the mountain home of William Hesketh Lever, the first Viscount Leverhulme, a native of Bolton, who founded the, still successful, firm of Lever brothers Limited. It is indicative of the popularity of this residence that many post card views still exist and a selection of these, plus photographs and information from various other sources have provided the foundation for this work.

The research and collection of pertinent information has proved a worthwhile, interesting and stimulating exercise. If the reader derives a like amount of pleasure from the following pages I shall be more than rewarded for my efforts.

Malcolm David Smith
Adlington, Lancashire
1983

Introduction

My intention is not to produce an exhaustive, detailed study of 'The Bungalow' because there is a natural loathing of technical books; but more a chronological story, illustrated by a collection of photographs, which I am sure will achieve more than the text. There are certain inherent difficulties in separating events into 'time bands' as, for instance, 'Roynton Cottage' and 'The Bungalow' existed between specific dates whilst Lever Park and the Bungalow Grounds were constructed over a long period of time, as will become clear.

I have experienced some difficulty in collecting information because whilst people are generally quite prepared to recount experiences or reminisce, there has been a marked reluctance to part with possession of material even for copying purposes. I met this type of obstruction on several occasions and the underlying reason was that those persons were afraid that the articles loaned would be lost or not returned to them which has apparently happened previously. Whilst mishaps do occur it is obvious that all the occasions were not accidental and whoever was responsible has rendered an extreme disservice. One can appreciate that a photograph for instance which has been in a family for a number of generations has great sentimental value and can be irreplaceable.

I have been fortunate enough to enjoy excellent co-operation from a number of people whose names I have included in the acknowledgement list, without assistance an undertaking of this nature is impossible and it would be naive to think otherwise. The list does not include all those persons to whom I am indebted for help because it is not practicable to obtain details of Library and Museum staff who are generally helpful in the course of their work.

Working on the adage, 'procrastination is the thief of time' I decided at the outset that on reaching a situation where the intelligence I was receiving became repetitive, it could well be because the information which was readily available had become exhausted. If there was then sufficient material to produce a cogent, chronological narrative this must be the optimum time to complete it. There is no doubt that much more is known about the place and a lot of photographic illustrations exist which will remain hidden, having been forgotten, or their significance has just not been realised, nevertheless I feel that there is sufficient included to afford the reader a reasonable impression and understanding of this interesting part of our local history.

The Friday preceding Easter Day is 'Good Friday' which is held as the anniversary of the Crucifixion of Our Lord on the cross at Calvary. It is an established custom amongst Christians to visit a high area of land on the anniversary of this date in token remembrance of Christ's suffering for us. The local venue for this annual pilgrimage is Rivington Pike.

Thousands of visitors roam the moors on Good Friday and many of them climb to the Pike Tower, an achievement in itself because, standing over one thousand feet above sea level, the Pike is officially classed as a mountain. I often went there as a boy, usually in a group, from the village of Coppull where I lived. We invariably got lost on the way but always managed to arrive, not too difficult considering that you can see the 'Pike' for miles around. I used to enjoy playing in 'The Bungalow' grounds which we knew as the 'Chinese Gardens'. Stories existed that a man used to live in a bungalow there but it was of very little interest to me either at the time or for some considerable period thereafter.

Living in close proximity to Rivington and seeing the bleak hills with their prominent landmarks in all seasons the familiarity does not breed contempt but inspires an affection which is difficult to describe. My interest in the moorlands secret was kindled by this affection and who could resist a 'mystery on the doorstep' so to speak.

Landmarks on the Moors above Rivington Village; left to right:
1. Independent Broadcasting Transmitter Mast – Winter Hill.
2. Pigeon Tower and Bungalow Grounds.
3. Pike Tower.

Chapter 1 – Landmarks

On a clear day, when mist or low cloud does not hide them from view, there are three distinct landmarks visible on the moors above Rivington Village.

The tallest and most striking is the Winter Hill Transmitter Station Mast towering above the Independent Broadcasting Authority Station on Winter Hill. The main mast has a number of sister masts adjacent to it but these are not always evident when viewed from the lowlands. At night time a series of red marker lamps arranged at intervals along its height are illuminated as a warning to aircraft.

Winter Hill is the highest point of the moors rising to almost 1,500 feet. In ancient times it was used as a site for certain religious ceremonies as Baines "History of Lancashire" records:–

> "The people assembled in Rivington to celebrate public worship in the open air at a place called Winter Hill, which, from its ampitheatrical form, exalted the congregation to hear the solemn truths thundered from the stone pulpit, which stood in its centre".

In more recent times a tragic aircrash occurred there on Thursday 27th February 1958, when a passenger plane flying from the Isle of Man to Manchester crashed into the hillside, in appalling weather conditions, killing all but seven of the forty two passengers and crew aboard.

The second landmark and by far the oldest is the watchtower on Rivington Pike. During the reign of Henry VIII (1509 – 1547) Rivington Pike was described by Leland as follows:–

> "one part of this Hille when I saw it first is called Faierlokke, but communely the people thereabout caulleth it Riven pike";

and he adds,

> "There was a Coppe in the Hille, as a backe standing up above the residue of the Hille".

The 'coppe' was the site of an ancient beacon, one in a chain extending the length and breadth of England, maintained for the purpose of sending messages of alarm in times of danger. (The building of the Beacon Tower on Rivington Pike – G. N. Shawcross).

The earliest mention of the beacon on Rivington Pike dates back to 1588 when during the reign of Elizabeth I, whilst England was threatened by invasion from the Spanish Armada; the fleet assembled by Phillip II of Spain for the conquest of this country, the beacon site was continually manned for several months – "to appraise the inhabitants of the approach of the invaders and to rouse into action their most vigorous efforts". The cost of manning the site was shared between the divisions of Manchester, Bolton and Middleton. (Baines History of Lancashire).

*Rivington Pike Tower circa 1880 from a photograph by Luke Berry of Chorley. (Note Chimney).
Seated in front are Mrs. Margaret Evelyn Crompton with her two sons Andrews and Theodore.
John William Crompton is standing in the centre of the group to the left. This family occupied
Rivington Hall until 1910.*

The present watchtower was built in 1733 and stones from the ancient beacon were incorporated at the base of the construction. A story is attached to the building of the present tower which is briefly as follows:–

In 1729 John Andrews of Little Lever, Bolton who owned one half of the Manor of Rivington, by descent, purchased the other half from one John Breres for the sum of £1,747.

The landlord of adjoining property, Christopher Horrocks, had proceedings brought against two of Andrew's employees for allegedly taking and detaining a cow at a place called Wildersmoor on the 17th March 1733.

The dispute centred on where the moor boundary lay between the respective properties of Andrews and Horrocks. The two accused employees were strenuously defended by Andrew's legal representatives. Litigation became both protracted and costly and in the event the action was dismissed in 1737 after three hearings at the Assizes. The outcome however resulted in the moor boundary between the parishes of Rivington and Horwich being properly defined".

John Andrews commenced negotiations with local stonemasons to build the present watchtower on the 17 June 1732. The accounts for the building work published by Shawcross make interesting reading. For example:–

May 1733 – paid James Gill for making cellar – 17 daies and ½ and he is to doe one day more at covering the Sough for that wage – £1-00s-05d.

The Beacon Tower is 20 ft. high and 17 ft. square externally. The interior is a single chamber 13 ft. square and a fireplace was included in one corner. Entrance was on the east side and there were windows in each wall. Cellar accommodation was 5 ft. deep by 3 ft. square under the 3 in. thick flag floor which was supported by stone buttresses. It

may be said that John Andrews erected the tower as evidence of legal ownership of the moor.

The structure was intended as a hunting lodge and the protective warmth which it afforded against the bitter winds will no doubt have been most welcome to the hunters. During 1933 when Shawcross wrote his article on the tower he recorded that the exterior of the building had been recently pointed and was in good condition although the roof had decayed and over half the covering had fallen into the main chamber. A few years ago the dangerous state of the watchtower prompted discussion on the advisability of having it demolished but following a public outcry Chorley Rural District Council took over the responsibility to renovate and preserve it for posterity.

Looking at the western slopes of Rivington Moor there is a roughly square shaped area of dense vegetation covering a section of the hillside laterally and extending almost to the summit of the moor. This concentration of trees and shrubs stands out as dark green against the paler hues of the coarse shrubs and grasses which cover the remainder of these uplands and appears incongruous to the observer. The explanation is that within the perimeter of this area stood 'The Bungalow' set in 45 acres of beautifully landscaped gardens, which dwelling has been described as "one of the most attractive small residential properties in the North of England".

In the top left hand corner of this square of vegetation standing like a lonely sentinel silhouetted against the skyline, is the third of these landmarks, the 'pigeon tower'.

The barren and inhospitable spot chosen by Lord Lever as the site for his residence identified the need for animation to dispel the feeling of loneliness. This was introduced by building bird houses throughout the grounds, whose feathered inhabitants cheered up the place with their constant comings and goings amidst a cacophony of sound.

The 'pigeon tower' was built as a 'look out' and loggia were constructed below it with observation plateaux to take advantage of the panoramic views afforded from this altitude. Adjoining the tower was an arched opening with a screen 250 ft. long containing pigeon holes which relieve the otherwise unbroken face from monotony.

Of Italian design this 'Rapunzel' tower has rooms at three levels, access being gained by a winding stone staircase which runs up the semi-circular spine of the building. The two lower rooms were bird houses but the top floor was decked out as a small sitting room with a fireplace. Lady Lever is supposed to have spent many hours in the 'pigeon tower' sewing and playing musical instruments, not very well though I am told.

That anyone should contemplate living in these wild and rugged surroundings, let alone conceive the idea of constructing garden areas, where even the hardy moorland shrubs and grasses barely managed to exist, seems totally incomprehensible; but all of this and even more was eventually achieved, principally due to the vision and courage of a singularly brilliant individual, William Hesketh Lever; a native of Bolton to whom I shall refer more fully in subsequent chapters.

The Pigeon Tower stands above the loggia and the boating lake. Lord Lever sometimes went for a swim in this small lake.

Chapter 2 – Rivington Hall Estate

Although Rivington is not specifically mentioned in the 'Domesday Book' there is little doubt that it existed as a manor before the Norman Conquest in 1066. In the Great Inquest of 1212 reference is made to 'RUHWINTON' in the Salford Hundred which was held in 'thanage' by Alexander Pilkington. The title 'Ruhwinton' is an early name from which 'Rivington' was derived. A 'thane' incidentally, in the Anglo-Saxon community was a member of the class intermediate between tenant farmers and the nobility. His property was held on condition of military service and required the payment of a nominal annual rental of a few shillings to the Crown.

The illustrious Pilkington family who fought at the Battle of Bosworth Field during the Wars of the Roses, and were almost wiped out, have contributed much to the history of Rivington. Their family crest includes a man with a scythe and the motto "NOW THUS – NOW THUS" which is an allusion to one of the family who, in order to escape his enemies, disguised himself as a mower. Richard Pilkington was responsible for the building of the first Rivington Church and his son James, who was born in 1518, became Bishop of Durham, the first protestant prelate of this see.

The Non Conformists of Rivington built a Chapel for themselves in 1703 where they could be a united congregation, free to manage their own affairs, and, above all, free to worship God according to the dictates of conscience.

Robert Pilkington was the last Lord of the Manor of Rivington from that family. He is reported to have borrowed considerable sums of money on the security of his lands and by his will, dated 16th November 1605, he left the estate in trust to three executors who transferred it to the mortgagees in settlement of the debts. Robert Lever of D'arcy Lever and Thomas Breres of Preston, bought out the various claimants and between them acquired the Rivington Estate. The two property holders passed their lands to surviving issue until; as previously mentioned, John Andrews bought out the other remaining tenant in 1729.

In 1834 Lucy Fletcher, a descendant of John Andrews, married Woodhouse Crompton of Bolton and thus the name of Crompton enters the lineage. Their son John William Crompton married and the couple had two sons, Andrews and Theodore. During the 1890's this family decided to sell Rivington Estate and R. Cecil Winders, Solicitors of Bolton were engaged to act in the negotiations.

Coincidentally Lord Lever was on the 'look out' for a suitable property in the area and on hearing that Rivington Hall Estate was on the market he was immediately interested in purchasing the lands. He had loved the moors since his childhood days and had enjoyed many happy hours there during his courtship with Lady Lever.

In January 1900, Lord Lever instructed a local firm of solicitors, F. W. Thompson Esq., of Wood Street, Bolton to negotiate the purchase of Rivington Manor. An opening offer of £40,000 was made but this was rejected as being nothing approaching the sum which was acceptable to the vendor. As the initial offer was rejected Winders were asked to provide a valuation figure for the estate which was eventually put at £70,000 and the sale included an agreement that John Crompton could occupy Rivington Hall, at an agreed annual rental, and his wife, and eldest son Andrews after him, if they so desired.

Objections were made to Andrews continuing in residence, for obvious reasons, and following the withdrawal of this condition Lever's solicitors made a firm bid of £60,000 which was accepted on the 23rd March 1900.

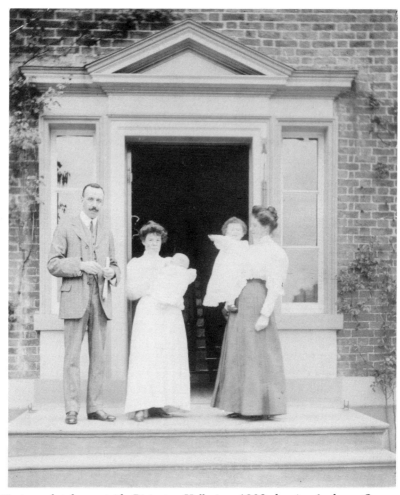

Photograph taken outside Rivington Hall circa 1908 showing Andrews Cromp-ton with Mrs. Crompton (on right) and a maid servant holding the Crompton children.

The formalities were concluded and Lord Lever became Baron of Rivington Manor whilst the Crompton family retained occupation of Rivington Hall, including the stable and coach-house; Sweetloves Cottage, Sheephouse Cottage and a vegetable garden near Fisher House, for a yearly rental of £100.

In studying the correspondence concerning this transaction, which is held in Bolton Library Archives, one sentence suggests that John Crompton was unaware of the prospective purchaser and this seems to have been done in an effort to obtain the estate at the most reasonable price. Had Crompton known that Lever was the prospective buyer he may well have insisted on the full asking price of £70,000, knowing that the latter could well afford it. The sentence which I am

Successive tenants had rebuilt the Hall on two occasions. Firstly in 1480 when Robert Pilkington built himself a more spacious abode, quadrangular in shape and constructed of timber and plasterwork; and secondly in 1780 when this building had decayed to such an extent that it was demolished and replaced by the existing Manor House.

Lord Lever's agreement to rent the Hall means that he must have intended to build an alternative residence and the site chosen for it, at 1,000 feet above sea level, on the western slopes of the moorland, is reputed to be a favourite picnic spot which he regularly visited with his wife-to-be during their courtship days. No account seems to have

Rivington Hall circa 1910.

referring to appears in the letter of acceptance and reads:–

"Is there any reason now why your client's name should not be disclosed to Mr. Crompton. We should like to do so".

The Rivington Hall Estate extended over 2,100 acres and included the manorial seat, Rivington Hall, a number of farmstead holdings, two Anglo Saxon tithe barns and, of course, the watchtower.

been taken of the vicious winds which can assail this elevated spot. It was an aspect probably viewed as unimportantly as it was during those halcyon days of early romance.

A better understanding of Lord Lever's motivation to build a home on that lonely fell side is achieved by a study of the antecedents and character of this remarkable man.

Photograph of Lord Leverhulme circa 1924.

Chapter 3 – William Hesketh Lever

William Hesketh Lever was born in Bolton on the 19th September 1851, the eldest of two sons in a family of ten children.

His mother and father were hard working people who ran a thriving wholesale grocery business in Bank Street, Bolton. They were strict Non-Conformists, totally opposed to drink or gambling but nevertheless the family enjoyed a happy childhood and were devoted to their parents.

William received his primary education at a small private school in Wood Street, Bolton, a pleasant Georgian cul-de-sac where the family home was also situated. The school took boys until they turned nine and girls up to sixteen years of age. The friendships which William formed at this establishment were to remain throughout his life, he had the good fortune to enjoy the companionship of his school friends in old age.

Educationally speaking William was not the most gifted pupil but he proved to be quick witted, resourceful, orderly minded and diligent, with a keen interest in sport particularly swimming. He left school when he was sixteen years old, his last school attended being a Church of England concern; which was a little unusual considering the religious persuasion of his parents. On leaving school he was taken into the family business being treated without preference and paid the 'going rate' of one shilling per week for cutting up the long bars of soap into manageable sized pieces and wrapping them in waxed paper.

Involvement in the day to day workings of the family enterprize caused William to react against his father's business conservatism. He suggested a number of administrative and procedural changes to improve efficiency which were initially viewed with some misgivings but on their being implemented they proved to be of great benefit.

A single and relatively insignificant sixteenth birthday gift had a deep and lasting effect on William. He was given a copy of the book 'Self Help' by Samuel Smiles which had been first published in November 1859. The book contains a series of anecdotes concerning the lives of such famous people as Richard Cobden, Robert Peel, Isambard Kingdom Brunel and Lord Nelson.

The message which this work conveys is that all things can be achieved by purposeful application and economical usage of 'time'. The point is emphasised in that the famous personages mentioned have made their mark in history despite their upbringings, which were often in poor or deprived circumstances, and the constant trials and tribulations encountered in the quest for success. I have read a copy of the book which is a little 'dry' but the quotations, two of which are repro-

Portrait of Sir William Hesketh Lever Bt. by George Hall Neale.

Portrait of Lady Lever by Mrs. Maud Hall Neale.

duced below, when read in conjunction with the biographies, are very valid:–

"An economical use of time is the best method of securing leisure: it enables us to get through business and carry it forward, instead of being driven by it. On the other hand, the miscalculation of time involves us in perpetual hurry, confusion and difficulties; and life becomes a mere shuffle of expedients, usually followed by disaster. Nelson once said, 'I owe all my success in life to having been always a quarter of an hour before my time''.

"Useful and instructive though good reading may be, it is only one mode of cultivating the mind and is much less influential than practical experience and good example in the formation of character''.

The meteoric rise from the situation of a grocer's assistant, cutting up the long bars of soap into saleable size pieces and wrapping them, to being the owner of an internationally successful business concern with a multi-million pound annual turnover is too well chronicled to dwell on the mechanics of how the success was achieved.

William Hesketh Lever seized upon the idea of producing soap of the highest quality with the brand name 'Sunlight' and pursued this idea with unremitting assiduity, surmounting all obstacles along the way. The branches of his soap combine eventually extended to all parts of the world and he was personally and directly involved in their being set up, financed and successfully administered.

Everyone has heard of Port Sunlight the industrial village set up by Lord Lever during 1888. The first sod for the village was cut by Lady Lever with a silver spade, in March of that year, and this ceremony was followed by a celebration banquet at the Bear's Paw Restaurant in Liverpool. By January 1889 soap production had commenced at the new factory.

Although the roadways in this village were constructed long before the days of motoring the principal ones were 36 ft. wide with 12 ft. pavements on each side. A variety of architects were commissioned to design the houses in 'Old English' style. Residences were widely spaced and well appointed with all modern conveniences. It was a condition of tenancy that the person either worked for Lever Brothers or was entitled to a house for some special reason arising out of the business. The village is as interesting today as it ever was and I must say that I enjoyed my visit there whilst researching this undertaking.

The fruits of his labour were vast but he was a generous man evinced by the numerous benefactions he made of which it would be impossible to give an exhaustive list. His intimate association with Bolton meant that the township benefitted in several ways. Bolton School was the outcome of a £100,000 gift from Lord Lever in 1912 and Hall i'th Wood Folk Museum, the home of Samuel Crompton, inventor of the spinning 'mule', was also equipped and given by him. Lever Park and D'arcy Lever Park were other donations along with numerous paintings and works of art to form the nucleus of collections at several public galleries.

His one partial failure was on Lewis in the Hebridean Group of Islands off the West Coast of Scotland which he bought in 1915. Efforts to increase the material prosperity of the inhabitants by helping them to develop local crafts and improve their fishing industry met with considerable opposition from the crofters. Lord Lever was finally forced to abandon his plans there during 1923 giving away 'Lews Castle' which had been his home.

He enjoyed better success on the Island of Harris, in the same group where the islanders responded to his schemes for improvement and the port and town of 'Leverburgh' commemorate his beneficial enterprise.

A very meaningful existence resulted in recognition not only from Great Britain but from other countries to where Lord Lever's soap combine had spread. His principal title was bestowed during 1922, when he was created a Viscount and chose to be 'Viscount Leverhulme of the Western Isles'.

This brief account gives some idea of the type of individual who became Lord of Rivington Manor and who has left such a fine legacy for so many to enjoy.

Lord Lever's Coat of Arms.

19

The Portable Building Co
46a, Market St. Manchester.

SHOOTING BOX WITH TILED ROOF ERECTED AT RIVINGTON FOR W·H·LEVER

Promotional advert issued by manufacturer's of 'Roynton Cottage'. The illustration is misleading because it gives the impression that the building was sited much lower down the hill.

'Roynton Cottage' shortly after erection: Work on the gardens had not commenced at this stage.

Chapter 4 – The First Bungalow 'Roynton Cottage'

Being precluded from occupying Rivington Hall, having agreed to its rental to the Crompton family, Lord Lever immediately put in hand the plans which he had for the construction of an alternative residence. His choice of dwelling was a little uncharacteristic, considering the almost palatial properties which be owned in other areas, a sectional wooden building which he entitled 'Roynton Cottage'.

The Portable Building Company of 46a Market Street, Manchester were responsible for the design and construction of the first bungalow the sections of which were, most probably, delivered by rail to Horwich Station and then transported to the site by horse and cart.

As previously discussed the site chosen, on the 1,000 ft. contour of Rivington Moor, seemed totally inappropriate but may have been due to an affection which Lord Lever had for the spot. The type of building has also been the subject of some debate and two reasons have been advanced to show that it was only intended as a 'stop gap' measure. Firstly the pitch pine and red tiled roof 'hunting lodge' was assembled to afford Lord Lever a base on the site quickly so that he could personally supervise development; and secondly that he eventually intended to replace it with a more permanent and substantial dwelling in another part of the grounds, when things had become established.

'Roynton Cottage' was nevertheless, destined to remain although the original square shaped structure with its westerly facing aspect was to be altered and extended out of all recognition; chiefly due to Lord Lever's penchant for architecture.

A walled garden or 'garth' was constructed which adjoined the east side and was surrounded by 'Pergolas' – covered walkways formed of growing plants trained over trellis work. A circular stone dovecote was erected in the centre of the 'garth' with a bird bath at its base.

All modern conveniences were installed and the house was superbly furnished, its walls hung with tapestries, samplers, pen and ink drawings and family portraits.

The ground floor was almost doubled in area and a second storey was added transforming the 'hunting lodge' into that "More permanent and substantial dwelling", and thus removing the need to build a replacement. The cottage was fit to entertain royalty and Lord Lever was proud to invite his many influential and famous acquaintances to share his hospitality at 'Roynton Cottage'.

The tenant farmers on the Estate were not forgotten by the new landlord. On Saturday 9th January 1901, he presided at a dinner organised to allow them the opportunity of meeting him. All the farmers, their wives or the eldest son/daughter were invited and

THE FIRST BUNGALOW – ROYNTON COTTAGE

22

some 80 of their number responded. The guests were wined and dined in excellent style at the Black a'Moors Head public house, which was situated near to where Rivington Village Club now stands. They were entertained by a ventriloquist, a conjurer and a cinematograph exhibition was also given by Mr. Morris of Bolton.

As a point of interest the Black a'Moors Head was demolished in 1903 following persistent complaints from the Liverpool Water Authority that the inadequate provision of sewage disposal facilities was resulting in pollution of the reservoir.

Several events were in progress at one and the same time, the improvements to 'Roynton Cottage', the laying of the bungalow grounds, the setting up of a system of roadways throughout the Estate which connected with the existing transport routes and the gift of Lever Park.

'Black-a-Moors Head' public house known locally as 'The Black Lad'. It was demolished in 1903.

I have already referred to the improvements taking place to the bungalow and will discuss the grounds and roadways later but the gift of "Lever Park" is a complicated subject which I shall now endeavour to explain.

'Roynton Cottage'. View across the lawn at the north front showing a gardener at work. (Circa 1906).

'Roynton Cottage'. Telescope at the west front.
The telescope mounting was inscribed with the
names of places visible from this spot. (Circa 1905).

'Roynton Cottage' Bowls game in progress on the lawn. (Circa 1907).

Rivington Hall Estate comprised 2,100 acres and it was Lord Lever's intention to dedicate approximately 400 of those acres as a public park for the benefit of the townspeople of Bolton and the surrounding district.

In September 1901, Lord Lever left England on a voyage to Australia, but a few days before sailing he arranged that during his absence representatives should convey his offer of the park to Bolton Corporation.

His generous gesture was contained in a letter reproduced below:–

J. Simpson Esq.
F. W. Thompson Esq. and
Messrs Hulton, Son & Harwood, Bolton

Thornton Manor
Thornton Hough
Cheshire

6th September 1901

Dear Sirs,

I shall be obliged if you will communicate to the Mayor of Bolton on my behalf an offer to give to the Town of Bolton a portion of the lands in the parish of Rivington belonging to myself, which are enclosed within the undermentioned boundaries and more clearly shown on accompanying plan, to be used as a Public Park for the use and enjoyment of the Public for ever, but subject to the understanding that during my lifetime I may, provided same be done at my own sole expense, erect on such land any building or buildings for the use of the Public, or make any roads or footpaths thereon for the proper opening up of the land for the use of the Public and generally deal with the land as may appear to me to be desirable for the purpose for which the Park is intended, viz. its free and uninterrupted enjoyment by the Public.

BOUNDARIES:– A line drawn from the Black Lad in Rivington up Sheep House Lane, down Hall Lane, up the north side of Hall Wood to Old Kate's following the south east side of Hall Wood to the contour line at 600′ above sea level as shewn on the ordnance map, following approximately the 600′ contour line to the Douglas Brook in Shaw's Clough and then following the Douglas brook until the same reaches the Rivington Reservoir.

Within these boundaries there are other properties which do not belong to myself, and which of course are not included with the lands I am now proposing to give.

I also offer on the same conditions Rivington Pike, within the following boundaries:– On the north and north east side within the contour line at 1150′ above sea level; on the south and south west side within the contour line at 1125′ above sea level; and also sufficient land along the line of the two footpaths leading from the high road to the Pike, and measuring from the centre of said footpaths 60′ on each side, to make each of these approaches 120′ wide.

It will necessarily take some time before the land can be dedicated to the use of the Public, and in bringing this about I particularly wish that every consideration be given to the farmers and others who are tenants upon the estate, and that every reasonable care be taken to cause the minimum inconvenience.

If the Town of Bolton is pleased to accept this offer, I shall be obliged if you will take the necessary steps to have the property transferred, so that the matter may be completed on my return home in December next.

Yours faithfully,

W. H. Lever

Lord Lever's offer was gratefully accepted on behalf of the people of Bolton and the way seemed clear for things to progress on all fronts but storm clouds were gathering on the horizon to thwart the advance.

Liverpool Corporation Water Authority had the opportunity to buy Rivington Hall Estate before Lord Lever became interested and even after the latter had completed his negotiations with Crompton he gave the Corporation an option to purchase at the agreed price but they declared no interest in being landowners.

In the spring of 1902 Liverpool Corporation promoted a Bill before Parliament to obtain powers to acquire certain areas comprised in the Rivington watershed including the Estate which Lord Lever had bought. The Bill came before a Select Committee of the House of Commons on the 1st May 1902 and the Corporation were granted a compulsory purchase order for the lands with the exception of some forty five acres which Lord Lever could retain as the curtilage of his dwelling, with certain restrictions, and the proposed park was to remain as such and be known as "Lever Park".

'Roynton Cottage', terracing immediately below the bungalow. The four gabled pigeon tower is of short squat design in this photograph and was later replaced (Circa 1910).

The only question to be resolved was the price which Liverpool Water Authority should compensate Lord Lever for his lands and wishing to avoid further expensive litigation the latter suggested that he be paid the purchase price of £60,000 plus his expenses to date. This was refused and, as no mutually acceptable arbitrator could be agreed upon, an umpire was appointed by the Board of Trade.

Following investigation Lord Lever was eventually awarded a sum which was almost double the amount he had paid for the whole Manor. In spite of an appeal by the Water Authority the judgement was upheld and left "egg on the face" of the Engineer-in-Chief whose 'opponent's' name was to be perpetuated on lands belonging to Liverpool Corporation.

The uncertainity of the outcome of these proceedings meant that work was delayed to some extent but some progress had been made on both the bungalow grounds and the municipal park. Having covered the major developments to 'Roynton Cottage' it now remains to tell the story of its total destruction by fire.

'Roynton Cottage'. A second storey was added shortly before it was destroyed by fire – the familiar twin gables became a trio. (Circa 1912).

Lord and Lady Lever can be seen standing behind the boys on the Great Lawn (Circa 1907).

Lord Lever addressing boy scouts and members of the boys' brigade from the Summer House on the Great Lawn.

Chapter 5 – Suffragist Outrage

1913 was a particularly unfortunate and sad year for Lord Lever. He was then in his early sixties and might reasonably have been expected to be thinking in terms of easing the pace of his business life, by delegating responsibility to his subordinates and spending more time with his wife and son. This was not to be the case however because subsequent events robbed him of the opportunity as we shall see.

In the early part of this century women did not enjoy the status or liberty most do nowadays. There was no question of a female Prime Minister being elected or the "Sex Discrimination Act" reaching the statute books. The 'weaker sex" were subjugated in a male dominated society where they were considered merely as chattels. Protestations at the injustice of the situation were treated as something of a joke.

Tired of a 'milk and water' approach to improving the lot of womankind a number of gifted and articulate females formed themselves into the Suffragette Movement, which was, in effect, an early form of the Women's Liberation Movement. The leading lights of the society were Emmeline and Christabel Pankhurst who campaigned actively and vigorously for the right of women to vote in government elections. They even suffered terms of imprisonment in the fight for what they saw was their right.

Edith Rigby, wife of Doctor Charles Rigby of Winckley Square, Preston, was 40 years of age in 1913 and an active supporter of the Suffragette Movement. The life story of this very individual and determined lady is chronicled in an interesting publication entitled "My Aunt Edith", written by her niece of course who is Phoebe Hesketh, a local authoress and poet. Mrs Rigby had joined in many of the protest meetings and marches organised by the Suffragettes and had also served a number of terms of imprisonment for more militant activities. Imprisoned members of the cause continued to protest by going on hunger strike but a most devious counter measure by government agencies caused much suffering amongst their number. The measure referred to was to confine the hunger striker until her health had deteriorated to a dangerous state and then release her. Following recuperation and convalescence outside prison she was re-arrested to serve the remainder of her sentence. This was a most inhuman piece of legislation referred to as the "Cat and Mouse Act". The harsh treatment meted out to the Suffragettes resulted in a hardening of resolve and indirectly led to the more serious manifestations of militancy.

Late on Saturday night, the 5th July 1913, there was a terrific explosion in a cafe underneath Liverpool Cotton Exchange. A

Edith Rigby of Winckley Square, Preston who admitted the arson attack on 'Roynton Cottage'.

piece of piping a foot long and an inch and a half in diameter was found to have contained explosive packed with stones and pieces of iron. No person was injured but considerable damage was caused to the Exchange. This incident is linked with the arson attack on Roynton Cottage, both acts of vandalism being later admitted by Edith Rigby.

Plans for the attack on the bungalow were carefully laid and executed as follows:

"Albert Yeadon, a resident of Preston, had been enlisted as an accomplice in the conspiracy to further draw attention to the plight of women. Yeadon's wife was allied to the Suffrage cause. Ironically, Edith Rigby needed the assistance of a strong man to carry the full paraffin containers to the site of Roynton Cottage.

About noon on Monday 7th July 1913, cans of paraffin were loaded into the boot of Doctor Rigby's motor car at Preston, and Edith Rigby together with Albert Yeadon, were driven to Rivington by the family chauffeur. The latter was totally unaware of what was intended. On arrival at Rivington the paraffin was unloaded and the chauffeur was dismissed to await the return of his mistress and Mr. Yeadon who then made their way to the bungalow grounds.

It had been ascertained, possibly by calling at one of the barns for refreshment, that no person would be in residence at Roynton Cottage on this particular day; which seems to confirm that there was no intention of causing death or injury to persons by the attack but strictly to cause damage to property. (It will also be remembered that no person was injured in the explosion at the Liverpool Cotton Exchange).

Having carried the paraffin to within easy reach of the bungalow Edith Rigby said she wanted to complete the plan herself and asked Yeadon to leave and wait for her in the car. Edith walked around the bungalow checking that there was no one inside and started fires at several places by breaking windows and pouring paraffin through before igniting it with a taper. In the dry summer conditions the wooden bungalow was a veritable "tinder box". The fire soon took hold as Edith made her way back to the waiting transport.

The report in the Bolton Journal dated 8th July 1913, suggests that 'Roynton Cottage' was fired around midnight, which may or may not have been the case. A watchman connected with the Liverpool Waterworks first discovered the fire about 1.30 am. on the 8th July and aroused Mr. Adamson the residential engineer for the Waterworks who lived in close proximity to the bungalow. He quickly dressed and on reaching the site saw the bungalow burning fiercely in three or four places on all sides of the building, the separate seats of fire tending to suggest "Arson". It was obvious, even at that stage, that Roynton Cottage was doomed, the pitch pine boards of the dwelling were well alight and night breezes were fanning the flames which raged out of all control.

Tenants of the lodges attached to the Estate were alerted and telephone calls were made to summon the Fire Brigade. Mr. Adamson spoke firstly with the Horwich (Lancashire and Yorkshire) Fire Brigade and later the Chorley Brigade were contacted but neither attended because Rivington was outside their recognised boundaries. Chief Officer Semple of the Horwich Brigade attended unofficially about 2.30 am. and directed the fire fighting efforts.

Alderman James Lawrence J.P. of Anderton Hall, which was situated directly across the Lower Rivington Reservoir from Roynton Cottage, saw the flames and telephoned the Fire Brigades at Horwich and Chorley. He could not contact the latter so he got out his motor car and drove there only to receive the same answer given to Adamson earlier. Realising the importance of informing Lord Lever, Alderman Lawrence telephoned "Thornton Manor", his Lordship's Cheshire home.

In July 1913 King George V and Queen Mary were making a Royal Tour of industrial Lancashire and spent the evening of Monday 7th July as guests of the Earl and Countess of Derby at Knowsley Hall. Sir William and Lady Lever were amongst the guests invited to dine with Their Majesties and left the Hall in the early hours of the morning.

It was 4.00 am. on the 8th July, when Alderman Lawrence contacted Thornton Manor. Whether Lord Lever had then returned home or was still detained at Knowsley Hall is not clear but the information was eventually communicated to him and amongst the many expressions of sympathy which he received at the loss of his beautiful Rivington home was one from the King which read:–

> "Much regret to learn from newspapers that while you were here last night (Knowsley) your house at Rivington and its contents were destroyed by fire. I sympathize with you in your loss – George R.I.

The dreadful irony was that Lord Lever was in favour of Women's Suffrage.

Several clues were left to indicate that the fire was the work of the Suffragettes. A small dispatch case left in the grounds contained a typewritten message which read:– "Lancashire's message to the King from the women, 'Votes for women due' – Message to the King, Liverpool: Wake up the Government. First give us reason to be loyal then try us".

The case also contained a pair of lady's grey suede gloves one of which was gashed across the palm and blood stained.

Edith Rigby pre-empted a successful enquiry when she gave herself up to the police in Liverpool on Thursday 10th July admitting both the explosives attack on the Liverpool Cotton Exchange and the arson outrage at Rivington. Insisting that she was solely responsible the explanation given for the Cotton Exchange attack was because of a grievance in that the great cotton industry of Lancashire was built up on women's labour and whilst the merchants were willing to get power and wealth from that labour, women were denied the vote.

On being remanded in custody for these offences Edith Rigby made the following statement from the dock:–

> "I want to ask Sir William Lever whether he thinks his property on Rivington Pike is more valuable as one of his superfluous homes occasionally to be opened to people, or as a beacon lighted for King and Country, to see that here are some intolerable grievances for women". (Manchester Evening News 10th July 1913)

The remains of 'Roynton Cottage' following the arson attack.

Although the loss of Roynton Cottage was a bitter blow, Lever determined to replace it with a more substantial residence and the second bungalow was thus planned to rise as a "phoenix from the ashes". It was to be constructed of stone and concrete giving little chance to the incendiary.

On the 19th July 1913 Lord Lever left to inspect associated companies on the continent. Most unusually he travelled without his wife who had social engagements at home. Whilst in Marseilles he received a telegram informing him that his wife was gravely ill and managed to reach her bedside just before she drifted into unconsciousness and died on the 24th July.

This shattering blow totally eclipsed the loss of 'Roynton Cottage'. Lord Lever had first met his wife, then Elizabeth Hulme, when they attended the small private school in Wood Street, Bolton together as children. Their childhood friendship had blossomed into a deep and lasting love and they were married in 1874 being blessed with a son.

Following the death of his wife Lord Lever paid this tribute to her:–

"It would be a poor compliment to my late wife if I left you under the impression she was a business woman, that she would make suggestions about the business, and suggestions about building the village and other institutions. She was essentially a womanly woman, and her knowledge of business was nil. But I always told her, as soon as I knew myself exactly how the business was progressing, and I can say, after full and careful thought, that I am convinced that without her influence there would have been neither a Port Sunlight, nor a Lever Brothers as we know it today. It came because of the confidence she inspired in me.

During the whole of our married life of forty years, however early business called me, I never breakfasted alone; she was always up and saw that the breakfast was properly prepared, and I always knew that whatever might happen in the course of the day the great event for her would be my homecoming in the evening.

Behind and before all our religion stands the home; Civilisation is founded upon the home; the centre of the home is the wife. A wife need not be an inspired genius in guiding and directing her husband. Genius might be a handicap and not a help – but she can be an inspiration and source of confidence the greatest inspiration to me had been the wife I was fortunate enough to win".

The loss of his closest companion had a deep and lasting effect upon Lord Lever but he determined to overcome his grief by keeping it a personal matter and committing himself with renewed vigour to his multifarious activities.

As a memorial to his wife Lord Lever erected the 'Lady Lever Art Gallery' in Port Sunlight Village. The building was opened on the 16th December 1922 by Princess Beatrice and remains an interesting place to visit.

Three wooden 'pagodas' around the Japanese Lake were used as 'tea houses' on visiting days. Rice paper covered the windows as protection from the breezes and at night on these special occasions illumination was provided by copper lamps hanging from the 'pagodas', lamps in the stone ornaments and strings of electric light bulbs around the shores of the lake.

Chapter 6 – The Bungalow grounds

Roynton Cottage existed for only a dozen or so years before it was destroyed by fire and I have covered the full sequence of events in the two preceding chapters in order to avoid confusion. It will be appreciated that the cottage, grounds and municipal park were developed in roughly the same time span and I will once again deal with events separately in order to afford the reader a clearer impression.

View of the Lancashire Plain across the Japenese Lake (foreground) and Lower Rivington Reservoir (middle distance). The replica of the ruins of Liverpool Castle is on the near shore (right) of the reservoir.

View across the 'orchestra' lawn. The sun dial – top left – was sited on a favourite picnic spot of Lord and Lady Lever during their courtship. The photograph was most probably taken from the flat roof of 'The Bungalow'. (Circa 1925).

Looking across the boating lake from the Loggia below the Pigeon Tower.

"In order to overcome the sloping angle of descent the gardens were laid out in terraces".

Harold Dickinson – haulier of Horwich – transporting stone for the construction of Rivington 'Dell'. The lead horse, named 'Nigger' was used on active service during the 1914 – 18 war. (Photograph circa 1920).

Construction of waterfalls in the 'Dell'. The water course was diverted during building.

Workmen in the 'Dell' – approximately 100 men were employed during construction – the foreman, (extreme right) was a cockney named Fletcher. (Circa 1920).

As can be seen by the bridge this waterfall is the one shown under construction on the opposite page.

A lower section of the series of falls through the 'Dell'. Note how the bridge design differs from the one shown above.

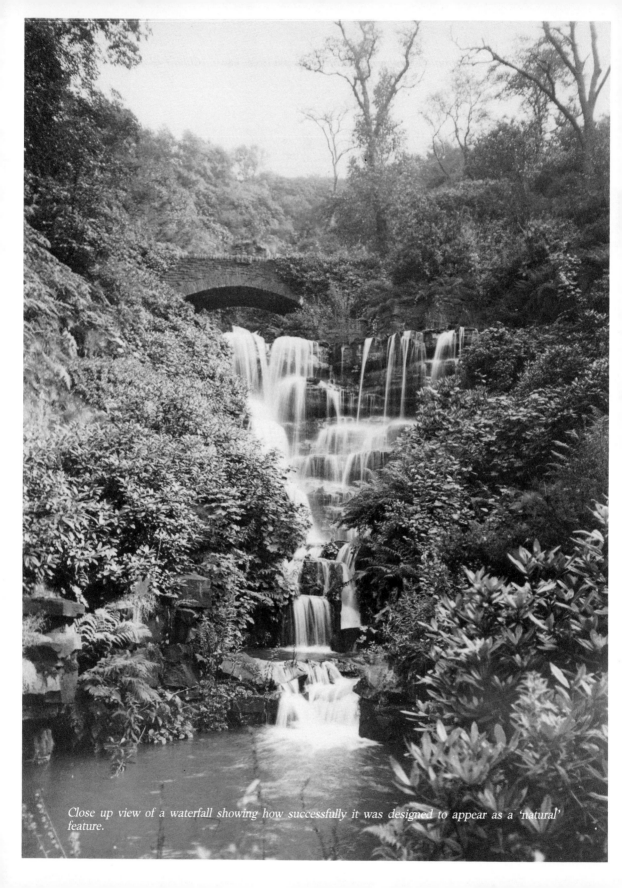

Close up view of a waterfall showing how successfully it was designed to appear as a 'natural' feature.

View of 'The Bungalow' from the pathway which divides the Great Lawn. (Circa 1925).

Entrance to Japanese Gardens near to Stone House Lodge.

A very attractive view of the Japanese lake taken shortly after its completion (Note the lack of vegetation). The stone ornament (centre) was cast in concrete and held a small lamp.

Below: Japanese Lake from above, there was a habitat for water birds on the far bank.

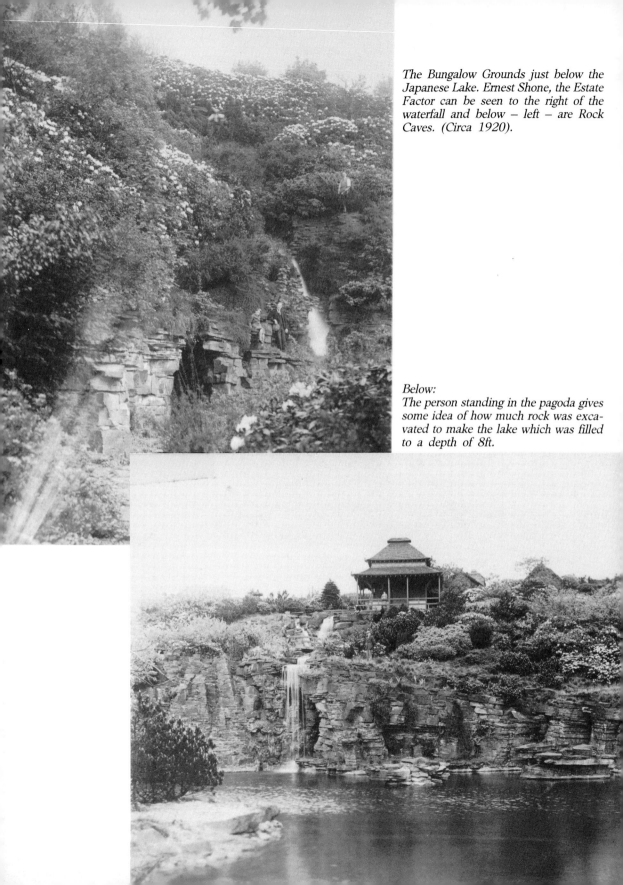

The Bungalow Grounds just below the Japanese Lake. Ernest Shone, the Estate Factor can be seen to the right of the waterfall and below – left – are Rock Caves. (Circa 1920).

Below:
The person standing in the pagoda gives some idea of how much rock was excavated to make the lake which was filled to a depth of 8ft.

'he Bungalow' from the Summerhouse
earest the Pigeon Tower.

Dense rhododendrons presently obscure this view of the Pigeon Tower from below.

The distinctive stone archway – right – is a good reference point for this scene across the Italian Gardens.

Having sited Roynton Cottage in such an isolated position the first priority was to establish lines of communication by road. This was achieved by widening and metalling existing moorland tracks and laying completely new stretches of road. Over twenty miles of roadway were eventually constructed which facilitated passage throughout the Estate and connected with the routes from Horwich, Bolton, Chorley and Belmont. The following quotations from the book "Viscount Leverhulme" written by his son, embody Lord Lever's attitude to road building:–

> "A friend, with home he was walking one day along one of the many roads which he constructed at Rivington, asked him why he was so fond of road-making. 'Well, for one thing', he replied, 'no one sees the ultimate usefulness of a road at the time I make it, and the result is no one thanks me for it'. 'The road-maker is the best anonymous servant of humanity'."

He said on another occasion:–

> "He drives a great broad thoroughfare from town to town, and for generations men travel over the road, with all their hopes and fears, with all their cares and joys, never once asking who it was that made their way easier for them. A road-maker's life is full of rich solitude and invisible rewards".

Following the assemblage of 'Roynton Cottage' work began on the grounds in earnest. The initial planning was carried out by local architects, most prominent amongst whom was Johnathan Simpson; Lord Lever's life-long friend from his schooldays in Wood Street, Bolton, he did not however make the most important contribution as we shall see.

Thomas Hayton Mawson was born at Scorton, a few miles south of Lancaster on the 5th May 1861, making him almost ten years younger than Lord Lever. Because Mawson was a delicate child his parents encouraged him to work in the gardens for both fresh air and in order to earn his pocket money. At 12 years of age Thomas went to Lancaster to work as an office boy and to learn drawing, building and horticulture but, after two years of this he returned to employment with his father in newly secured property at Bentham; where the family eventually set up a nursery and fruit farm. These events decided Mawson on a career in landscape gardening in which he enjoyed enormous success.

Lord Lever's meeting with T. H. Mawson was brought about, purely by coincidence, during the latter's attempt to obtain settlement of a debt. Mawson had designed a carved folding screen for his little church in Hest Bank and some part of the commission for the screen had not been paid. As Lord Lever was regarded a 'High Church Non-Conformist' Mawson wrote to him for a donation, enclosing a copy of the screen design. His Lordship was so impressed that he forwarded a sum of money and made the following request in his reply letter to Mawson;

Thornton Manor
Thornton Hough
Cheshire

Dear Mr. Mawson

I am very pleased to have the opportunity of sending you my cheque for the remaining carved panel in the screen of your beautiful village church and wish you every success in your endeavours still further to improve its services.

Now that you have had the courage to ask me for a subscription, may I be so bold as to ask you to come and advise me upon the improvement of my garden at Thornton Manor? I have wanted to consult you for the last two years, but all of my friends warned me that it would be useless, as you never worked for anyone holding less social rank than a Duke, whereas I am only a poor and indigent soap-maker. Let me know if you can come, and when, naming two or three alternative dates.

Your faithfully
W. H. Lever

After this first meeting during 1905 Mawson was extremely impressed with Lord Lever and described him as a "veritable Napoleon in his grasp of all factors dominating any problem to be tackled". He referred to Lady Lever as being "charmingly hospitable and careful for the comfort of her guests and always shed the radiance of a truly gracious spirit over the household". Lord Lever was equally affected with Mawson's qualities and was pleased to commission him for work on both the "Bungalow Grounds" and "Lever Park".

Lord Lever had already drawn the plans for a proposed layout of the bungalow grounds; as an amateur he said of himself; but Mawson said that they were truly remarkable. The estate was a planner's dream affording vast scope for individual expression and the 'frames of reference' supplied to Mawson were that the gardens should be "laid out in perfect keeping with their natural environment".

This summer house stood at the southern end of the walkway below the four gabled 'Pigeon Tower' opposite. (Circa 1908).

An excellent working relationship developed between Lever and Mawson; as the former never showed surprise or disinclination towards imaginative schemes proposed by the artist. The challenge of establishing garden areas on the barren, windswept moorland was seized upon by Mawson; the chief reason being that all his professional counterparts prophesied failure and laughed at the notion of anything other than the hardy moorland grasses growing there.

Experiments were carried out to find what types of flora the covering soil of the hillside would support. Nurseries eventually flourished with many varieties of rhododendron and peat loving shrubs, together with a host of other hardy trees and plants. The results far exceeded Mawson's expectations and fully justified the confidence which he had initially felt at the success of this venture.

The bedrock of Rivington Moor is sandstone which has an unusual horizontal stratification. This feature inspired the design work for many of the garden structures and proved to be as advantageous in the construction of the grounds as it had initially been envisaged preventative.

The situation of 'Roynton Cottage' prompted the need for shelter which was provided by means of the pergolas and garth, mentioned earlier, along with a host of little shelters, fitted with seating wherever possible; loggia and summerhouses.

In order to overcome the sloping angle of descent the gardens were laid out in terraces, crossed by wide, crazy paved walkways; and the various levels were connected by stone flights of steps.

Throughout his life Lord Lever enjoyed taking exercise whether it was swimming, walking, horse riding or a work out in the gymnasium. For him a garden was not a place to 'stand and stare' but for brisk promenading hence the long sections of walkway. The pergolas incidentally were constructed to form two L's (Initials of Lord Lever) and were specifically to allow him to complete walking exercises during inclement weather.

Rivington Pike from the Western Shore of the Japanese Lake.

The grounds are divided into two sections by the roadway which runs from Sheephouse Lane, under 'Lord Lever's Bridge' and connects with Old Will's Lane, behind Rivington and Blackrod High School. The upper section contained 'Roynton Cottage', the pigeon tower and loggia, a number of lakes, a series of miniature waterfalls, the lawns, shrubberies and Japanese Gardens. The lower section is largely wooded with waterfalls cascading through it. Four pathways run horizontally across this section at different levels which include bridges spanning the chasm of the largest waterfall from the Japanese Lake. A flight of 365 steps gives access through the lower gardens, which number signifies the days in a year as the four pathways are meant to represent the four seasons.

The lawn at the north front of Roynton Cottage is reputed to have been turfed with 'springy' grasses brought from Scotland. In the corner farthest from the house was situated a sundial which recorded the time accurately enough to be reliable. On the dial was a plate inscribed 'LIVE TODAY, NOT REGRETTING YESTERDAY NOR FEARING TOMORROW'. Diagonally opposite the sundial was a flight of semi-circular 'orchestra' steps connecting with the bungalow. On a fine evening the musicians played on the steps whilst guests used the lawn for dancing. Games of bowls, tennis and croquet were also played there.

Gardeners at work in the Bungalow Grounds.

Terracing ran along the verandah at the west front of the house and a large telescope, mounted on a stand, stood on the terrace. On a clear day it was possible, with the aid of this telescope to see as far south as the Welsh Mountains and as far north as the Lake District Hills. The names of places visible were engraved on the mounting for the telescope.

A range of greenhouses including a lean to fernery extended behind Stone-House Lodge. These were heated and the vegetable produce grown there amply supplied the bungalow kitchen with fresh produce. At the far end of the hot houses was a 'bothy' or small cottage, used by the gardeners for potting plants, storage of implements, warmth, shelter etc.

View along the walkway below the Four Gabled Pigeon Tower. (Circa 1915).

A remarkable feat of excavation resulted in the construction of the great lawn situated about one hundred feet below the site of Roynton Cottage. This lawn is divided into two unequal parts by a crazy paved walkway which itself splits and runs along the top edge of each lawn. In addition to a number of small shelters there was a summerhouse adjacent to the pathway, in each part of the lawn. I am indebted to the staff of the Information Centre at Port Sunlight for allowing me to copy a number of photographs two of which particularly pleased me; one showing Lord Lever addressing a group of Boy Scouts and Boys Brigade members from a summerhouse, and the second was of him on the lawn standing with these boys and their supervisors.

In the largest half of the great lawn, some 325 yards long, a portion of the underlying rock was left at its natural level and clearly shows the enormous tonnage of material which must have been removed during the making. This chunk of rock stands almost seven feet above the grass level.

Lord Lever's business ventures entailed a number of trips around the world and he was often influenced by what he saw on his travels. His gardens bespoke architectural features of Italian and Japanese extraction.

There are two series of waterfalls in the grounds the design of which were derived from the hydraulic engineering feats associated with Italian formal cascades.

A 'miniature' series of waterfalls rise near the pigeon tower and fall into a small lake on each terrace. The first expanse of water in this line of descent is a lily-pond with a stone plinth in the centre on which there once stood a white stone statue of a boy standing on dolphins and blowing a horn; which seems to be an elongated sea-shell. This statue is known as 'King Neptune' but does not appear to me to depict this particular sea-god. The second lake which these falls plunge into is much larger and was used as a boating lake. Water birds also made their homes in the banks of this pool adding to the interest.

A small stream which meandered through a leafy dell divided the grounds into two, almost equal parts. This rill was temporarily diverted whilst the sandstone bedrock was quarried to form a second series of waterfalls. A natural effect was achieved by using the quarried stone for construction work; the result being so successful that it is difficult to distinguish between the natural sections and the man made. Two single arched stone bridges were thrown over the chasm of the waterfall to connect the two halves of the garden and because the original stream was of insufficient force to warrant the cascades which had been engineered a number of feeder streams were also diverted to augment the flow.

An unusual feature of this stairway is that it divides to form a square.

This white stone statue of a boy and dolphins was known as 'Neptune'. The easily recognisable plinth can still be seen.

51

Bridge over the waterfall in the lower part of Rivington Dell.
View of Lever Park looking across the parapet of Lord Lever's Bridge

What is now known as the 'large lake' in the Japanese Gardens was in fact a compensation reservoir for the waterfalls during dry weather conditions. The lake and waterfalls employed 100 men in the building and railway lines were laid to assist in moving the vast quantities of rock. Further stone was brought from a nearby quarry using horse and cart transport which was verified by the haulier contracted to do some of this work; Harold Dickinson of Horwich, who kindly allowed me to copy photographs.

The Japanese Lake has a concrete base and can be filled to a depth of eight feet. It was possible to empty the waters of the lake in 30 minutes by means of a penstock which was opened by a wheel locked away in a wooden hut hidden amongst the shrubbery. This was only done on isolated occasions but the surging waters descending the cataracts below were a magnificent sight.

The Japanese Gardens were laid following an idea from Lord Lever inspired by the 'Willow Pattern Design' and later extensive personal research in Japan. This design was introduced into England by Thomas Turner of Caughley about 1780 and the following is the tale which has been built round it:–

"A wealthy mandarin had an only daughter named Li-chi, who fell in love with Chang, a young man living on the island shown, who had been her father's secretary. The father overheard them one day making vows of love under the orange-tree, and sternly forbade the unequal match; but the lovers contrived to elope, lay concealed for a while in the gardener's cottage and thence escaped in a boat to the island. The enraged mandarin pursued them with a whip, and would have beaten them to death had not the gods rewarded their fidelity by changing them both into turtle doves. And all this occurred 'when the willow begins to shed its leaves'".

Standing on a bridge in the Japanese Gardens are Joseph Henry Shone and Margaret Shone parents of Ernest Shone. (Circa 1930).

The lake was the focal point of these gardens containing small rocky islets on which were situated stone ornaments, others were dotted about elsewhere in the grounds. Three wooden pagodas were erected around the lake which during visiting days were used as tea houses and had their windows covered with rice paper shutters to keep the breezes at bay. At night copper lamps hanging from these pagodas were lit to give the gardens the appearance of 'fairy land'. A story exists that the stone pathways running through the Japanese Gardens convey a message, to the initiated at points where they turn or junction.

Exotic flamingoes, swans and wild ducks found a home on the lake and completed the overall impression intended of a Willow Pattern scene. One can almost imagine the enraged Mandarin chasing the lovers across a bridge in these gardens, the doves which abounded throughout the grounds in those early days would doubtless add to the illusion.

Archway in stepped walk before the gardens were planted. (Circa 1906).

Just before Lord Lever's death excavation work started to convert part of the Great Lawn into a second lake to increase the head of water to the falls. The railway track (left) was built to facilitate movement of stone. (Circa 1925).

54

...lian Loggia as seen from the boating lake. Seating was provided both inside and on the observation plateau.

Visitors on the steps leading to the summerhouse (1920).

...ne for relaxation on the observation ...ateau of the Loggia shown above.

Caves and grottoes were 'erected' in the Dell by using a similar technique to that employed in building the cascades, i.e. by partial excavation and using the excavated material for construction work. It was intended to put bears in the caves but this idea never came to fruition.

The following anecdote shows how well Mawson had laid the gardens to blend in with their natural surroundings:–

"One day Lord Lever was showing a friend round the gardens when the latter remarked, 'It must have been a big task to cut that path through the little hill'. Lord Lever smiled and explained that, as a matter of fact he had made the path first and then, built up the hills on either side of it".

The size of the bungalow grounds, extending to over 45 acres, make it impossible to discuss each and every feature; but I feel sure that the illustrations included along with the written description are sufficient to convey the breathtaking beauty of these "Hanging Gardens of Rivington".

'Roynton Cottage' from the terrace below the 'Pigeon Tower' with Belmont Lodge far left. (Circa 1910).

Chapter 7 – Miscellany

I have deliberately omitted to mention a number of important features of the grounds in the previous chapter in order to afford them special mention and hopefully give the reader a clearer understanding.

Lodge Houses

Lord Lever owned several properties, the three principal ones being "Thornton Manor", Thornton Hough, Cheshire, "The Hill" at Hampstead, London, and 'The Bungalow", Rivington, Lancashire. The situation of Port Sunlight in Cheshire and the fact that London, being the capital city, was the centre for business and commerce, meant that he had greater occasion to occupy the two former homes. 'The Bungalow' was more of a pleasant country retreat for him although he held a special affection for the place.

Absences from his property in Rivington for such long periods prompted the need for resident staff who could maintain the estate and provide security for the many valuable art treasures kept there. In 1906 Mawson was asked to construct gatehouses at "Roynton Cottage" as well as the "pigeon tower". Bolton, Belmont and South Lodges were built of double weather board walling with thatched roofing. They were sited at the respective entrance points to the bungalow grounds and each comprised: Sitting room, kitchen, scullery, pantry, bathroom, toilet and two bedrooms. It seems that South Lodge, situated at

the entrance from Rivington Lane, was the "Cinderella" of the three because it was not fitted with either central heating or electric lighting, but was nevertheless a very comfortable and spacious abode. Stone House Lodge was built about 1915 and was of unusual design in that the entrance drive ran right through the centre of it. As the name implies it was stone built with a slate roof and consisted of sitting room, kitchen, scullery, pantry, bathroom, toilet, three bedrooms and two cellars.

The estate's main employees occupied the lodge houses and I was able to speak to Keith Shone who lived at Stone House Lodge, his father being employed as the 'Estate Factor'; and Jack Kings who moved into South Lodge with his parents in May 1926 when his father secured employment as a gardener on the estate.

Lever's Bridge

A popular feature of the grounds is Lever's Bridge which spans the road running from Chorley to Horwich. Mr. Kings recounted a story that Lord Lever asked his chief stone-mason, Edward Hart, to build a bridge over the road incorporating seven separate arches. Not fully understanding what his employer meant Mr. Hart commented that the road was too narrow to be spanned by more than one arch, whereupon he was instructed to pack a suitcase for a journey the following day. On joining His Lordship as asked Hart found himself on an Imperial Airways flight bound for Nigeria, where, on arrival he was shown a bridge which spanned a narrow gorge and was told to copy the design for the one intended at Rivington.

The architectural details of the 'Romanesque' style bridge are purely attributable to Lord Lever, who knew exactly what he wanted; and I can think of no finer way of conveying his wishes than by showing his workman the actual design to be copied, albeit an expensive 'visual aid' to construction.

(My wife's grandfather, Paul Fairclough, was a stone-mason and worked on building projects in the bungalow grounds walking to the site from his home in Babylon Lane, Anderton.)

Sadly the original plans for the bridge were lost in the arson attack on 'Roynton Cottage'.

Top right:
Stone House Lodge was built about 1915 and was of unusual design in that the entrance drive ran right through the centre of it.
Bottom right:
South Lodge – The 'Cinderella' of the four lodge houses, being without central heating or electricity.
Below:
Visitors to 'Roynton Cottage' circa 1906. (Belmont Lodge is in the foreground).

The Motor Car

Since 1885 when the two German engineers, Karl Benz and Gottlieb Daimler, independently produced vehicles powered by an internal combustion engine, with petrol as fuel, the development of the motor car has been very rapid. Early vehicles were slow, open to the weather, and gave a bumpy ride due to the tyres being solid.

Lord Lever was an early user of the motor car and owned quite a number of vehicles. On long journeys he often took two cars so that he could stop from time to time to transfer into his own vehicle one of a group of people travelling in the second car, all of whom he wished to interview on various matters. This allowed him to fully utilise every minute of his time and is true to the principles and tenets of Samuel Smiles.

The excellent roadways which Lord Lever had constructed made Rivington a popular venue for motor trials and vehicles often took part in hill climbing competitions along the estate roads.

Stables, Garages and Power Plant

At the north east corner of the bungalow grounds, almost opposite the pigeon tower, there is a recess cut into the hillside which has the appearance of a disused quarry. This area is presently used as a sheep pen but it once contained the stabling and garage accommodation and the generating plant for Roynton Cottage.

With the rise in popularity and use of the motor vehicle some of the stabling was converted to house motor transport. Eventually there were two stone built heated garages sufficient to accommodate four

Lord Lever's seven arched 'Romanesque' style bridge.

Bolton Lodge from the Lower Drive leading to the front of 'The Bungalow'. The original 'Thatched' roof proved impractical and was replaced by tiles.

vehicles. One of the garages was fitted with an Inspection Pit. There was also a detached petrol store built nearby.

Lord Lever always had a passion for horse riding and became a familiar figure on his early morning rides through the leafy Rivington Lanes. The stabling for his animals comprised a four stall stable with loft and a two stall stable. The stableman had a room provided above a harness store.

The electricity generating house was situated near to the garages and power was supplied by means of a 10 h.p. National Paraffin Engine.

61

Lord Lever on horseback visiting a scout camp at Rivington. (Circa 1907).

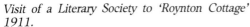

Visit of a Literary Society to 'Roynton Cottage' 1911.

General Amenities

A telephone system was installed at both Roynton Cottage and Belmont Lodge, the telephone number incidentally was Horwich 28 which I considered as a suitable title for the work at one stage.

The water supply was piped from a spring near Winter Hill and both hot and cold water were on tap at Roynton Cottage and the Lodge Houses. The water supply was heated by coke fired, 'Robin Hood' boilers situated in the cellars and central heating was provided by radiators. Drainage for the property was by the 'Septic Tank Principle'.

Open Day – A band plays on the top of the summer house near the Great Lawn and even though it is raining the ice cream seller manages to attract children. (Circa 1930).

Open Day – Visitors descending the steps from the Pergola onto the 'Orchestra' lawn. The group right of centre is approaching the sun dial. (Circa 1930).

'Open Days'

The bungalow grounds were essentially private property and metal fencing was erected around the perimeter. It was not until the summer of 1919 that the general public were allowed an 'open day' being charged a nominal sum for admission, the whole proceeds being donated to charity. Almost 4,000 visitors attended on this occasion, benefitting local charities to the amount of £77.4s. 5d., and this initial success resulted in the exercise being repeated over the next five years.

The public were allowed free and unrestricted access to 'Lever Park' the second major landscape commission which Lord Lever entrusted to T. H. Mawson.

Open Day – Visitors on the Great Lawn. (Circa 1930).

Open Day – The summer house and loggia had observation plateaux where visitors could take advantage of the views.

Lever Park near to Rivington and Blackrod Grammar School (left) – Lever Park Avenue had not been constructed at this time.

View of Lever Park Avenue with Pike in background. (Circa 1950).

Chapter 8 – Lever Park

I have already explained a number of the steps leading to the development of Lever Park but feel it prudent to recapitulate in order to give continuity.

Rivington Hall Estate extended over 2,100 acres and Lord Lever offered 400 of these acres free to Bolton Corporation, for use as a municipal park, in September 1901.

Liverpool Corporation, most probably alarmed at this proposal, promoted a Bill to secure certain lands on the Rivington 'water shed' including Lord Lever's Estate. Litigation ensued which resulted in the Water Authority being granted power to acquire lands in the Rivington drainage area with the exception of 45 acres which Lord Lever was allowed to retain for his bungalow and grounds. The proposed plans for a 400 acre public park were upheld and it was to be named "Lever Park". Liverpool Corporation obtained free possession of this particular land because it was a 'gift' but were to permit Lord Lever, at his own expense, to lay out the area for the use and enjoyment of the inhabitants of the County Borough of Bolton and generally of the public for ever.

Arbitration followed respecting the amount of compensation to be paid for those lands compulsorily purchased which resulted in the Water Authority being ordered to pay almost double the price which Lord Lever had initially obtained the whole estate for.

These proceedings were not finally resolved until May 1905 although the first judgement was made during May 1902.

Following the acceptance of the gift of 'Lever Park' work began on its conversion for such use in June 1902. The object was to make the park "as free, as accessible and as attractive to the townsmen of Bolton and the public in general, as possible".

Suitable access was provided by roads, the next question being shelter for the thousands of visitors. This problem was solved with two immense Saxon tithe barns, Rivington Hall Barn and Great House Barn. Jonathan Simpson, Lord Lever's local architect, was contracted to restore them for use and succeeded in putting the two structures into a thorough state of repair by reconstructing them in keeping with their original beam rafters and stonework. Kitchens were provided where large numbers of the public could be served with refreshments at moderate prices.

The Crompton family left Rivington Hall and moved to Cheshire following the death of John W. Crompton. This mansion of the former squires of the estate was converted into a Picture Gallery and Art Museum and opened to the public free of charge.

Plan
OF
THE BUNGALOW,
RIVINGTON,
LANCASHIRE.

Scale of Chains.

Links 100 0 1 2 3 4 5   10   20   30   40 Chains

NOTE—This Plan is based upon the Ordnance
Survey Map with the sanction of the Con-
troller of His Majesty's Stationery Office.

Martin Hood & Larkin Photolitho Gt. Newport St. W.C.

'The Bungalow' from Lever Park – South Lodge is bottom left. The Pigeon Tower is top left and Belmont Lodge is top centre.

Exterior view of Great House Barn from Rivington Lane.

Interior view of Great House Barn.

Interior of Rivington Hall Barn.

Rivington Hall Barn shortly after it was renovated. (Circa 1904).

Programme for the Opening Ceremony of Lever Park.

Beech House Rivington with 'Roynton Cottage' on the skyline.

View of Lever Park with Wood's farm to the left.

Closer view of Wood's Farm.

Beech House from the slopes of Rivington Moor. Anderton hall stands opposite across the Lower Rivington Reservoir.

Rivington Hall Farm.

Rivington & Blackrod Grammar School. (Circa 1914).

'The Clog',
Anglezarke.

(now demolished).

Higher Derbyshires Farm,
Lever Park, Rivington.

Knowle House,
Lever Park, Rivington.

Trees were planted beside the newly constructed roads, fields were fenced and a number of paddocks were erected stocked with deer, buffaloes, emus, yak and many other animals. A herd of Chartley cattle were introduced which are the original native breed of these Islands.

A small lake in front of Rivington Hall was divided into two by constructing a road through the centre of it which connected with Great House Barn. Black swans from Western Australia were introduced to the eastern section of the divided lake and white swans to the western half.

The whole impression was that of an 'open air zoo' and it is easy to imagine the delight and wonderment of visitors on seeing, most probably for the first time in their lives, such unusual animal and bird life. It was appreciated however that the chief interest was in the green fields and open spaces where people could wander at will, take 'al fresco' meals or merely 'sit and stare'.

Lake in front of Rivington Hall before it was divided by the construction of the roadway leading to Great House Barn.

Group of bystanders admire a black swan gliding across Rivington Hall Lake after it was divided.

Lever Park was first opened on the 18th May 1904, when at 1.15 pm. that day W. T. Mason Esq., M.A., a former Headmaster of Bolton High School for Boys formally conducted the ceremony outside the entrance to Rivington Hall Barn in front of a large and representative gathering. Four trees were planted to commemorate this event and luncheon followed in the Barn where entertainment was provided.

There was still much work to be done on the park and the commission was granted to T. H. Mawson, as discussed previously, following his meeting with Lord Lever in 1905.

Sam Winstanley, assistant keeper, with lioness cub in Lever Park.

Zebras in 'Lever Park'.

Liverpool Corporation were consulted at every stage by Lord Lever's representatives and voiced no opposition to his plans. In retrospect there was no reason why the issue could not have been solved more amicably without invoking the acrimonious arbitration. There is little doubt that ignorance of the full facts meant that Lord Lever's standing was far less in Liverpool than elsewhere which was a dreadful pity because he was forced into a situation against his will and reacted in a reasonable and rational way.

The following quotation from the work "Lord Leverhulme" by W. P. Jolly hints at a possible explanation:–

"It is remarkable how often Lever seemed to bring out the worst in public officials. Sometimes it almost seemed that they resented the way he achieved instant reforms by spending his own money, when they were struggling to do much the same using public funds".

Liverpool Castle was the first nucleus of the City and was eventually demolished to

Presentation to Rev. W. Ritson, vicar of Rivington Church and Mrs. Ritson on their retirement in 1918. Lord Lever is centre right of the group outside Rivington Hall Barn.

Aerial view of the replica of the ruins of Liverpool Castle built on 'Coblowe' by the eastern shore of Lower Rivington Reservoir.

Liverpool Castle

make way for commercial development. As a final touch to Lever Park a replica of the ruins of Liverpool Castle were erected on a hillock known as "Coblowe", which is situated on the eastern side of the Lower Rivington Reservoir. Work was commenced on the ruins about 1912 but proceeded slowly employing only a handful of stonemasons and labourers. The plans were never finally completed and work ceased after Lord Lever's death. The ruins were a bold experiment in landscape design and the result, after the newness of the stonework had worn away and become covered with moss and lichen, was eminently successful.

Lever Park was virtually completed in 1911 and with all due ceremony the Park was officially dedicated for use by the public on the 10th October that year. The workforce and villagers celebrated with a luncheon and dance in Rivington Hall Barn whilst the main guests enjoyed their own luncheon and speechmaking in Rivington Hall.

The principal features of Lever Park are as popular today as ever they were. Rivington Hall and the two Barns still host social functions and refreshments are available at the Barns during weekdays. A small aviary exists near to Rivington Hall stocked with a variety of birds but the animals have long since departed. The replica ruins of Liverpool Castle remain an enigma to those unaware of their history. The effects of nature have so mellowed the structure that it appears as a totally authentic ruin which was what the builder intended.

Chapter 9 – The Second Bungalow

There is always some good to come out of evil even if it is only that the knowledge of how and why tragedy occurred can assist us to avoid or prevent a repetition in the future. The fact that Roynton Cottage was a timbered dwelling exacerbated the losses incurred and so Lord Lever determined that the replacement would be structured of stone and reinforced concrete which materials at least would be non-combustible.

Fortunately the first bungalow was covered by insurance and the compensation monies would go some little way towards the cost of re-building. Two other aspects of the fire loss which could be considered beneficial were, firstly that Roynton Cottage was not totally in keeping with the unique gardens which had been landscaped around it as they bespoke an even finer residence; and the opportunity was presented to build a magnificent replacement. Secondly the devastation felt by Lord Lever at the loss of his wife needed an outlet and the architectual challenge of designing the second bungalow was irresistible. It provided him with the opportunity to occupy his mind on positive ventures and thus lessen the pain of his inner grief.

Throughout his life Lord Lever had a genuine love of architecture which was due to his interest in art. This was officially recognised in 1918 when he was appointed an Honorary Fellow of the Royal Institute of British Architects.

A friend said of him:–

> "The love of the beautiful in art and nature has always been a strong feature in his judgement and taste".

His son said of him:–

> "Altering the face of nature was with him a passion. He was never happier than when seated in front of a plan with a drawing-board, ruler and 'T' square ready to hand. Architecture was always an absorbing study for him, and one can safely say that no single man – at any rate in modern times – has ever built a larger number of houses and buildings and constructed a greater mileage of roads. With him it was never a case of leaving everything to the architect and settling the bill when the work was finished. Expert advice he wisely sought and freely acknowledged, but the plan and lay-out of Port Sunlight were his own, and so, in the main, were the plans for the works and buildings in the village, and in many cases of the houses also. The architects he employed all looked upon him as unique amongst their clients. He did not employ them – he collaborated with them".

Lady Lever commented that she seldom experienced the sensation of living for very long in a house free from the presence of workmen.

In 'collaboration' with Lord Lever, Jonathan Simpson designed a single storey replacement bungalow constructed of stone with random coursed walling in conformity with the ancient Lancashire traditions; the flat roof being of reinforced concrete giving little chance to the incendiary.

'Roynton Cottage' had a westerly facing aspect which left it open to the fiercest assaults of the prevailing winds and so 'The Bungalow' was sited facing south. Any intention which Lord Lever may have had to re-position his dwelling was precluded once the grounds became so well established.

The garth and pergolas were incorporated as an integral part of 'The Bungalow'; which name Lord Lever has chosen for his new home. It is difficult however to imagine a more inappropriate title because the planned dwelling was far removed from the popular conception of a bungalow being more in keeping with a 'country mansion'.

Little time was lost in rebuilding and within a year of 'Roynton Cottage' being burned to the ground, Lord Lever was in residence at 'The Bungalow'. A date stone commemorating the completion in early 1914 was included over the main entrance to the house.

South front of Bungalow 1918, before second storey was added. Note the Dovecote has not yet been sited on the grass island.

THE BUNGALOW RIVINGTON

In front of 'The Bungalow' where the driveways from Stone House Lodge and Bolton Lodge converge on the forecourt an old stone sign post was sited which gave the residence an air of antiquity. An interesting story is attached to this stone which is known as the 'Headless Cross'. The monument has the legs of a man on one face of the supporting stone and other designs on the remaining three faces. The square stone on top has the four sides carved with directions to Wigan (spelt with two g's), Bolton, Preston and Blackburn (inscribed Blagburn).

Above:
Dovecote inside the walled garden or 'Garth'. This was re-moved to the front of 'The Bungalow' when the Ballroom replaced the 'Garth' in 1922.

1st July 1924.

Mr. Shone,
Stone House,
The Bungalow,
Rivington,
Mr. HORWICH.

Dear Mr. Shone,

I am obliged for your memorandum of the 28th June and approve of your placing the white swan on the pool at the bottom of the Gorge until it can be put on the Japanese Lake.

With regard to the feeding of the swans, I prefer that Whittaker should continue to feed all animals, birds and fishes.

I am pleased to note that you have obtained the Headless Cross and three more stones from the pond at Ridgmont. I prefer all these relics shall be placed near the entrance to The Bungalow.

Yours sincerely,

Leverhulme

Left:
Lord Lever was kept informed of developments at Rivington. This letter was received by the Estate Factor and verifies the story concerning the 'Headless Cross'.

Joseph Ridgway who built Ridgmont House in 1809 was a collector of stone monuments and following his death in 1842 the 'collection' was neglected and fell into disrepair. Lord Lever had heard this story and asked Ernest Shone, the Estate Factor, to search the Ridgmont area for suitable stone. Shone located the "Headless Cross" by means of grappling irons, on a flooded section of the lands and the Cross along with base stones were recovered and sited in front of 'The Bungalow'. Following demolition the 'Headless Cross' was erected at its present position in Grimeford Village on the wide grass verge where Roscoe Lane Brow junctions with Grimeford Lane and Rivington Lane.

Winter Garden – west front – door on the flight right gave access to the lounge.

Winter Garden – north front – entrances between the fish tanks were to the Morning Room, Lord Lever's Study and Bedroom respectively.

'The Bungalow' largely comprised the following accommodation:–

Outer and Inner Halls
Dining Room
Morning Roon
Library
Study
Four Principal Bedrooms
Four Principal Bathrooms
Five Servants Bedrooms
Five Servants Bathrooms
Complete Domestic Offices

Inevitably it was altered on many occasions to suit Lord Lever's complicated idea of perfection; approximately one hundred alterations and improvements were carried out up to the time of His Lordship's death in 1925. R. Hermon Crook F.S.A., Architect and Surveyor of 17 Mawdsley Street, Bolton, successor to Johnathan Simpson, was responsible for designing much of the architectural change to 'The Bungalow'. Specialist contracts were of course undertaken by appropriate firms, the name of Robert Walsh, Plumbing and Heating Engineers appearing on plans for additions and alterations to the heating and hot and cold water supplies during 1920.

Dining Room – The lamp shade was made from sea shells collected from the South Sea Islands and was extremely lightweight. A plan of the Constellations of the Northern Hemisphere was delineated on the panelled ceiling.

1. *Pigeon Tower.*

2. *This Corner Building* contained the Aviary.

3. *Unglazed Pergola from the Cascade.*

4. *Pergola from North Front.*

5. *The Ballroom and Orchestra Steps from the Lawn.*

6. *North Front from the Sun Dial.*

GAMES ROOM

CONSERVATORY (NO ROOF)

CONSERVATORY (NO ROOF)

PERGOLA (TIMBER BEAMS – NO GLASS)

SEE PHOTO 3.

N

TOOL SHED

LADIES

GENTS

OPEN

(CONSERVATORY

CONSERVATORY

CONSERVATORY

SEE PHOTO 2.

PERGOLA – (GLASS ROOF)   SEE PHOTO 4.

SEE PHOTO 5.

SEE PHOTO 6.

ow' and Pergolas

NORTH EAST ELEVATION

William Hesketh Lever
– Viscount Leverhulme.

Front of Bungalow with Dove Cote taken from Small Pigeon Tower.

7. View from Lower Lawn of West Elevation and Small Pigeon Tower.

SECTION CT

GENTS
PORCH
ENTRANCE HALL
MAID'S BEDROOM
MAID'S BEDROOM
ALCOVE
LADIES
BATH
MAID'S BEDROOM
BALLROOM
MAID'S BEDROOM
T
ALCOVE
LOUNGE
HOUSEKEEPER'S ROOM
LARDER
BACK ENTRANCE
BEDROOM
BATH
ANTE ROOM
KITCHEN
SCULLERY
STUDY
BUTLER'S PANTRY
LINEN ROOM
STORE ROOM
MORNING ROOM
INNER HALL
OUTER HALL
GENTS
PORCH
BATH
BEDROOM
DINING ROOM
BEDROOM
BATH
BATH
LIBRARY
LOUNGE
BEDROOM

WINTER GARDENS – GLASS ROOF

MUSIC GALLERY
OVER VESTIBULE

FIRST FLOOR
(OVER HOUSEKEEPER'S ROOM)

BATH
BEDROOM
SITTING ROOM

BOILER ROOM
COAL CELLAR
CHUTE

CELLAR
(UNDER SCULLERY)

Both the main entrance and the servants' entrance were situated at the front of 'The Bungalow'. The beautiful solid oak doors were 'pegged' with wooden dowels and each door had two hinges at the top and bottom which 'wrapped' around the woodwork and were held in place by coach bolts.

'Upstairs' and 'Downstairs' quarters were in fact side by side at 'The Bungalow', the domestic section being entirely shut off from the main part of the house. All the main rooms were floored with polished oak or polished oak parquetry blocks, whilst the bathrooms, cloakrooms, secondary entrances and domestic offices had mosaic tiled covering. Italian craftsmen were contracted for the tiling and a special feature was that the edging tiles curved upwards where they adjoined the wall both to prevent dirt lodging and make cleaning easier.

Lord Lever's bedroom measured 19 ft. by 13 ft. and was fitted with a marble hand washbasin and heated towel rail. The whole of one side of the room was glass panelled and opened onto the Winter Gardens as did all the principal rooms in the house. A bathroom, gymnasium and tea room completed the master's suite. It was Lord Lever's

Inner Hall with roof light – fireplace alcove to the left with tiger skin rug.

custom to get up around 5.00 am. when he was in residence at 'The Bungalow' and due to his deafness, a 'Klaxon Horn' fitted over his bed doubled as his alarm clock. The sound of this infernal instrument not only managed to awaken him but also resident staff, the tenants of the Lodge Houses and half the populus of Rivington and Horwich in the process. Once out of bed he had a cold bath and exercised on a mechanical horse which 'shook' him dry. Twenty minutes in the gymnasium, a cup of tea and then dealing with correspondence until 7.30 am. was the start of his 'Working Day'. It seems that one of the secrets of Lord Lever's staying power was his ability to enjoy a short nap in the middle of the day.

There was direct access from Lord Lever's bedroom to the Study, the dimensions of which were 18 ft. 9 ins. by 12 ft. 8 ins. Leaving the Study along a short corridor one entered the Inner Hall measuring 45 ft. 6 ins. long by 21 ft. 4 ins. wide; the latter measurement included a deep recess which was fitted with an arched brick fireplace and tiled hearth.

Morning Room – Door right leads to Library. The glass partition extreme right opened onto the Winter Gardens.

Dimensions of the Morning Room which adjoined the Inner Hall, were 41 ft. 6 in. by 19 ft. 9 ins., which included a bay. A second arched brick fireplace with tiled hearth was fitted there.

The Dining Room was most impressive, the four roof support pillars being covered in plaster to disguise their function with a touch of neo-classicism. The panelled ceiling was decorated in blue and relieved by stars arranged in a plan of the Constellations of the Northern Hemisphere. Exclusive of two entrance recesses the room measured 36 ft. 10 ins. by 24 ft. 9 ins. and was fitted with a finely ornamented marble fireplace. The walls of the Lounge situated between the Dining Room and Winter Garden were hung with Japanese wicker.

A Library measured 19 ft. 6 ins. by 14 ft. 6 ins. and was fitted with bookcases the shelves of which were extremely well stocked. It had a polished oak floor and a pair of glazed doors led to the Winter Garden.

I was extremely pleased to obtain a ground floor plan of 'The Bungalow' which has made it much simpler to locate and explain the various rooms. By relating the plan to the text and illustrations included it is much easier to appreciate this well designed, functional and yet beautiful residence. The property was exceptionally well appointed with furnishings and art works of inestimable value. Lord Lever's arrangement of pictures and furniture was unerringly precise and balanced but he had a tendency to overcrowd. It was said of him that he furnished his rooms to be looked at rather than lived in.

Pergola extending from the orchestra steps towards the uncovered pergola. The archways led to the conservatories and were covered with ivy and roses. The end door led to an aviary.

Household staff enjoyed a high standard of accommodation similar in most respects to the extremely comfortable principal guest rooms. The kitchen was centrally positioned for convenience of service and was fitted with a double oven 'Eagle' range. There was also a heated linen room, butlers pantry, scullery, store room, larder and even a servants' sitting room. A telephone extension connected the butler's pantry with Belmont Lodge. All the principal apartments had electric bells fitted communicating with the kitchen where an indicator board alerted the staff that their presence was required.

The pergolas extending along the north and west fronts of 'The Bungalow' were glazed and the crazy paved walkways were carpet covered for warmth. Wisteria, Honeysuckle, Clematis and other varieties of climbing plant overhung the walkways and a series of fish or lily pools, enclosed by a pretty rock-like stone with centre fountains added further interest.

A spiral metal stairway gave access onto the flat roof of the dwelling which was fitted with sky-lights that had ventilation windows opening vertically thus allowing kitchen odours etc. to escape and preventing rain penetration.

The telescope which existed on the terrace of 'Roynton Cottage' was retained as a popular feature but was housed in a custom built observatory at 'the Bungalow'.

Apart from the Ballroom, which I will cover specially in the following chapter, the latest addition to 'The Bungalow' was an apartment for the housekeeper built over the servants entrance in the form of a second storey. It is thought that this functional suite had the dual purpose of shielding from view the dome of the ballroom when approaching the south front.

The cessation of hostilities in the Great War, waged to end all wars, saw the country in a celebratory mood following years of strife and there was a re-awakening of interest in dancing and social activities in general. Always abreast of the times, if not ahead of them, Lord Lever entered the 'Roaring Twenties' in fine style.

'The Bungalow' from the 'orchestra' lawn. The dome of the Ballroom Ceiling is visible extreme left.

Chapter 10 – The Last Waltz

During 1920 Lord Lever re-discovered the love of dancing which he had enjoyed in youth and early manhood. It held a threefold attraction for him firstly as a form of exercise, secondly as a means of entertaining visitors and thirdly it allowed him to indulge in what was essentially a youthful and light hearted pastime. Being almost 70 years of age he was conscious of what his contemporaries might think of this new found form of recreation and on one occasion he asked his son for a candid opinion. The reply was to the effect that there could be no possible harm in amusing himself in this way and absolutely no reason why it should provoke adverse comment. Grateful for this reassurance Lord Lever commented:–

> "Well the explanation is simply this: I spend the day entirely surrounded by men, and I don't want to spend my evenings also in ponderous conversation with men. I like to have a few young friends about me whom I can chaff. It keeps my mind young and prevents me from becoming dull and heavy".

The Ballroom was designed by R. Hermon Crook and replaced the 'garth' which was demolished to make way for it. The dovecote from the centre of the 'garth' was re-positioned on the forecourt in front of 'The Bungalow'.

Of circular design the ballroom was 44 ft. 6 ins. in diameter and the oak parquetry block floor was specially 'sprung' for dancing. (If necessary it could also be 'locked'). It can simply be described as a circle within a rectangle the latter being the area of the 'garth'. Of the four corners of the rectangle outside the circle's circumference two were used as alcoves, one as a lounge and lavatories were situated in the one remaining.

A glass dome in the centre of the ceiling gave light whilst the rest was decorated in blue and dotted with gold stars which were arranged as the Constellations appeared on the 19th September 1851, the date of Lord Lever's birth. This design was prepared by R. Hermon Crook.

Miniature fluted pillars supported the two fireside alcoves and they were fitted with finely carved oak mantels and jambs one of which came from the Island of Lewis. Keith Shone recollected that the latter mantel existed in a public house on Lewis and for generations local families had carved at a section apportioned to them. Lord Lever tried to buy the fireplace without success but eventually purchased the whole building just to obtain this desirable artefact.

Inside views of the ballroom included, convey much more of the exquisite furnishings than mere words. The beautifully carved gilt wood framed wall mirrors each side of the

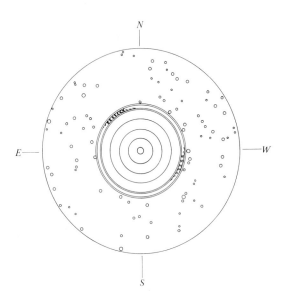

doorways and the intricate ornamentation above add interest. A pair of early Italian gates 3 ft. high by 6 ft. 6 ins. wide were positioned above the exit to the buffet/lounge and during 1923 a minstrels' gallery was built over the vestibule. A grill partially hid the musicians but the placement of the gallery meant that the dance floor was not obstructed.

Interior of the Ballroom. The ceiling was blue with gold stars arranged as the constellations appeared on the 19th September 1851, the date of Lord Lever's birth.

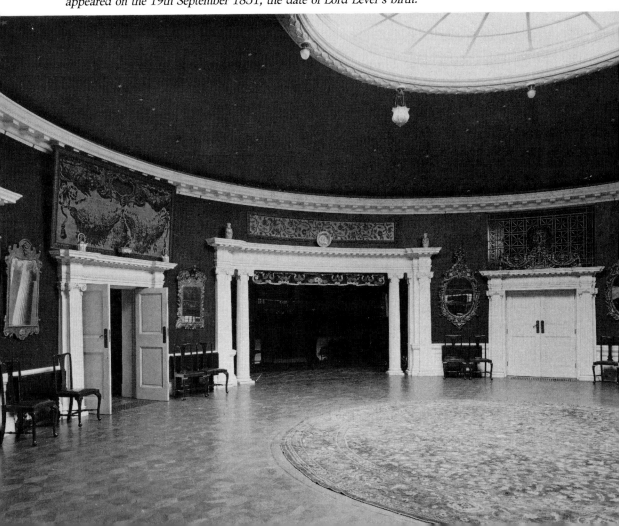

Hung on the wall of the ballroom was a Flemish Panel of unusually large dimensions (33 ft. long by 9 ft. wide). (During the sale of effects from the ballroom in 1925 this tapestry fetched £2,400, a considerable sum of money in those days). When not in use the ballroom floor was covered with a circular Persian carpet 19 ft. 6 ins. in diameter. This carpet was originally made in the harem of a Persian Prince and was bought from Lady Ratan Tata. The seating in the ballroom was provided by individual chairs arranged around the edge.

Portrait of Lord Lever by artist, Augustus John.

♔

Lord Leverhulme's

Fancy   Dress   Ball,

SEPTEMBER 30th, 1922,

Rivington Hall Barn.

◇◇◇

RIVINGTON PRIZE BRASS BAND
— AND —
LORD LEVERHULME'S PIPERS.

DANCING, 7-0 p.m to 11-30 p.m.

◇◇◇

Efficient M.C.s ::   REFRESHMENTS AT
                     REASONABLE CHARGES.

G.   Double Ticket - - 4/-.

Programme for a social function at Rivington Hall Barn.

His Lordship's deafness must have been quite a handicap on the dance floor. Even though he was an accomplished 'lip-reader' people wondered how he could follow the music or hear the start of a dance tune. It is reported that he had a small blue light installed in the ballroom ceiling which would light up and reflect in his patent leather shoes at the appropriate times; obviously switched on by an 'accomplice'. This simple device saved him some embarrassment and demonstrates his ingenuity.

Speaking of embarrassment, an amusing story is told by Lord Lever's son concerning a portrait which his father commissioned the celebrated Welsh artist, Augustus John, to paint in June 1920. When the work was finished at the end of August and despatched to His Lordship for approval he was less than flattered with the likeness of himself depicted on the canvas. Determined that no one should see the painting he immediately sent it for storage at 'The Bungalow', Rivington where it was his intention to hide it away in a safe. When Lord Lever came to store away

the offending painting it wouldn't fit so he cut out a square including the head, placed that in the safe and replaced the remainder of the painting into the packing case in which it had arrived.

Unfortunately his conscientious housekeeper noticing that the case was marked 'returnable' had it nailed up and forwarded to Augustus John. The artist was obviously surprised at receiving back his work in such a mutilated condition and contacted Lord Lever. The latter explained, quite frankly, what had happened and apologised for the embarrassing error. Although a little annoyed Augustus John accepted the circumstances but the Press got wind of the incident and the ensuing publicity led to a one day strike of artists in support of Augustus John.

The staff employed at 'The Bungalow' were charged with a great responsibility because the master was absent so frequently and for such long periods. Trips around the world and time spent at his other homes meant that Lord Lever only visited 'The Bungalow' intermittently for short stays.

During 1925, when 74 years of age, Lord Lever undertook a trip to West Africa against the advice of his doctors. The trip affected his health and friends noticed that on his return he did not look well even though he continued with his public duties.

On 27th April 1925, he travelled from Rivington to his home in Hampstead and the following day he was confined to bed with an attack of bronchitis. Despite a slight improvement pneumonia eventually developed and at 4.30 am. on Thursday 7th May 1925 Lord Lever died peacefully at his London home.

Tributes poured in from all parts of the world but on a personal level the staff and workmen employed at 'The Bungalow' were thrown into a state of uncertainty at the loss of their employer. Executors were appointed to administer Lord Lever's holding and it was eventually decided to sell Rivington Hall

LATE LD. LEVERHULME'S WILL.

GENEROUS BEQUESTS TO SERVANTS.

£1,000,000 VALUATION.

The will has been proved at a provisional valuation of £1,000,000 "so far as at present can be ascertained" of the late Right Hon. William Hesketh Viscount Leverhulme, described as "of the Western Isles, North Britain, and of The Hill, Hampstead, N.W.," the famous soap maker, chairman of Lever Bros. Ltd., and of Mac Fisheries Ltd., who died on May 7 last aged 74.

The will is dated September 11, 1924, and probate thereof has been granted to his son the Right Hon. William Hulme, now second Viscount Leverhulme, and Messrs. Harold Robert Greenhalgh, Francis D'Arcy Cooper, and John M'Dowell, company directors, all of Lever House, Blackfriars, London, to each of whom he left £5,000 for the executorship.

He left one-half of the total of fully-paid Ordinary shares in Lever Bros., Ltd., issued at his death (mentioned in an earlier statement as being 120,000 shares at £10 each) on trust for a period of 21 years after the death of the longest-lived survivor of his executors, his descendants living at his death, or the descendants of Queen Victoria living at his death, to pay three months' salary or wages for each complete year of service (no one bequest exceeding five years' wages or salary) to each of his domestic and personal staff on his private salary or weekly wages list, not being a co-partner in Lever Bros., Ltd., or under notice.

BENEVOLENT LIST NAMES.

To each of the following persons who shall be on his "private benevolent list" or "private benevolent pay list," an annuity equal to the amount of the pension paid by him at his death, viz., the Mesdames Scott, Watson, Warbrick, Orrock, H. C. Dickenson, and M. J. Johnstone; the Misses Dickenson, Taylor, Markland, and Dulston, and the Messrs. J. G. Davis, T. E. B. M'Donagh, and Henry Whittle, and the balance as to:—

10 per cent. to the chairman for the time being of Lever Bros., Ltd., for his own benefit.

10 per cent. on trust for the Viscount Leverhulme for the time being.

20 per cent. equally between the persons (other than the chairman of Lever Bros., Ltd.) constituting the Special Committee of Lever Bros., Ltd., except that the chairman of that committee is to be paid double the amount paid to each other member.

20 per cent. to persons (other than the chairman of Lever Bros., Ltd., and members of the said special committee) who shall be directors of Lever Bros., Ltd., or chairmen of any of the associated companies (i.e., a company not less than 9-10ths of whose issued ordinary capital shall be held by Lever Bros., Ltd.) in the following proportions:

"There shall be divided between the directors of Lever Bros., Ltd. (other than the chairman and other than the members of the said special committee), a sum which shall bear the same proportion to the total of the said 20 per cent. as the profits of Lever Bros., Ltd., available for dividend on the Ordinary share capital for the time being of that company for the financial year in respect of which the distribution of the said 20 parts is being made shall bear to the total of the said profits available for dividend on the Ordinary shares of Lever Bros., Ltd., and of the profits available for the dividend on the Ordinary shares of each of the associated companies for the same year, and to the chairman of each associated company such proportion of 20 parts as the profits of the company of which he was chairman bear to the total profits of Lever Bros., Ltd., and the associated companies."

FOR ARTISTIC ENCOURAGEMENT.

Twenty per cent. to the directors of the company "about to be incorporated by me for the purpose of acquiring Grosvenor House, to be applied by them for such purposes of artistic encouragement as the said directors shall think fit."

Twenty per cent. for such charities connected with commercial travellers, or grocers, or chemists, their wives, widows, and children (including in particular the London Commercial Travellers' Benevolent Society), and in such shapes and proportions as his trustees may see fit, any surplus not so applied being used for providing scholarships for such purposes of research and education (being valid charitable purposes) as his trustees in their discretion may direct.

At the end of the above period this sum is to be divided as to 30 per cent. to the Employes' Benefit Fund of Lever Bros. (Port Sunlight), Ltd.

As to 20 per cent. for the benefit of the Staff Training College of Lever Bros. (Port Sunlight), Ltd., as the trustees may think fit.

As to 20 per cent. to the directors of the Grosvenor House Company as above.

As to 20 per cent. to charities connected with commercial travellers or grocers or chemists, etc., as above.

As to 10 per cent. to the Viscount Leverhulme for the time being.

All other of his property he left to his son, the present Viscount Leverhulme. He declared that he made no provisions by his will for relations or friends because he had already during his lifetime made provision in all cases in which he had wished to do so.

He directed that his trustees should not be more than five in number, and that whenever possible they are to be directors of Lever Bros., Ltd., and members of the special committee of Lever Bros., Ltd.

Newspaper report on Lord Lever's Will – Daily Dispatch, Friday, July 10th, 1925.

Estate. Approximately one hundred workmen who had been carrying out improvements on the house and gardens were laid off leaving only the domestic staff and two joiners. The animals in Lever Park were offered to Bolton Council free of charge on condition that they would be looked after but many were eventually given to Belle Vue Zoo in Manchester or destroyed, the cost of keeping them being too prohibitive.

Messrs Knight, Frank and Rutley of 20 Hanover Square, London, were directed by the executors of the late Viscount Leverhulme to auction 'The Bungalow' and contents as well as the contents of Rivington Hall. At 2.30 pm. on Thursday 5th November 1925, the auction of 'The Bungalow' took place at the Midland Hotel, Manchester, and the property was purchased by John Magee of Magee Marshall and Company, Brewers of Derby Street, Bolton, for £15,000. The contents of 'The Bungalow' and Rivington Hall were auctioned in situ on Monday to Friday 9th to 13th and Monday and Tuesday 16th and 17th November 1925, from 1 pm. each day and John Magee purchased approximately £10,000 worth of goods.

The catalogue for the sale of the Leverhulme Collections contains 1,353 lots, including examples of old English furniture from Chippendale, Heppelwhite and Sheraton, antique needlework pictures, tapestries, paintings by many famous artists including Gainsborough, Sir John Lavery R.A., Erskine Nichol R.S.A., modern furniture, bedroom equipment, outside effects, motor vehicles etc. etc.

William Hulme Lever, D.Litt., succeeded his father as the second 'Viscount Leverhulme'. He was born on the 25th March 1888, being 37 years old on the death of his father. A married man with one son and two daughters he was then acting chairman of Lever Brothers Limited. It seems that the second Viscount had many things in common with his father except perhaps the same degree of affection towards that lovely, lonely moorland home, 'The Bungalow', Rivington, Lancashire. The son's affection for his father is evidenced by two tall polished granite pillars which stand at either side of the entrance to Lever Park, Horwich. They were erected in 1934 to commemorate the gift of Lever Park by his father and are appropriately inscribed.

Entrance to Lever Park Avenue marked by the two polished granite pillars erected in memory of Lord Lever by his son in 1934.

Chapter 11 – John Magee - The Second Owner

The new owner of 'The Bungalow' John Magee, was an entirely different personality than Lord Lever. His family ran the Magee Marshall Brewery Company Limited who operated from the 'Crown Brewery' in Derby Street, Bolton.

The firm was founded by David Magee in 1853 and the original brewery, completed in 1866 was considerably extended during 1875. Daniel Marshall ran a brewery in Brown Street, Bolton which Magee purchased in 1885 and three years later the joint concern was formed into a limited company.

Magee Marshall Limited were taken over in November 1958 by the old established firm of Greenall Whitley Limited of Warrington but the Derby Street Brewery continued production until the 2nd October 1970, when it was closed as part of a plan to increase the efficiency of production and distribution within the group.

Before the 1958 take over by Greenalls 250 licensed premises in and around Bolton, Wigan, Blackpool and Southport were controlled by Magee Marshall Limited. Their beer incidentally was brewed with water from Burton-on-Trent, 14 tank wagons, each carrying 60 – 90 barrels a time, regularly ran between Bolton and Burton-on-Trent where the firm had their own well and only the flowers of hops were used in brewing.

'The Bungalow' was intended for use as a week-end home by the Magee family and also as a sort of recreational and welfare centre for employees who were allowed to take advantage of the facilities for bowling matches etc. It was also decided to continue the practice of opening the grounds to visitors on occasions and allow the ballroom to be used for social functions.

After John Magee bought 'The Bungalow' the gardening staff was reduced to just five in number, one of whom was wholly employed in the kitchen gardens. Little was seen of the new owner at first except for brief visits using a company car for transport. As time went on his stays became longer so he bought himself a brand new Armstrong Siddeley motor car which he had delivered to his 'home' in Rivington. John Magee instructed Bob Whittaker, an employee who lived in Bolton Lodge, to act as his chauffeur and there followed a 'crash' driving course because he had never been behind the wheel of a car in his life before.

In spite of a marked disinterest at first the Magee family gradually grew to appreciate the amenities provided by 'the Bungalow' and it eventually became very popular amongst them and also the Co-Directors of the Brewery. A niece of John Magee, Miss Cynthia Weaver, prevailed upon him to have tennis courts laid at 'The Bungalow' so that she could indulge her passion for the game; and managed to persuade her uncle to use the smaller section of the Great Lawn for this purpose. Lord Lever had plans to convert this area of lawn into a second lake to provide a further head of water for the waterfalls but the proposal fell through after his death.

Contractors were employed in making two shale tennis courts, the first priority being the laying of an access road from the main drive. The work was done with pick and shovel, as the age of the 'mechanical digger' had not arrived, and on completion the estate gardeners were left to tidy and re-landscape the area.

The Directors of the Brewery were quick to realise the potential of the bungalow grounds as a ready source of materials to landscape the gardens and bowling greens of their more popular public houses. Once again John Magee was persuaded to agree to this suggestion. It seems that he was a benign, genial and somewhat absent minded man whose generosity it was easy to take advantage of.

One decision that John Magee made which he had cause to regret was to allow the local Hunt to hold their annual ball in 'The Bungalow' ballroom. The event degenerated into a drunken revel and so much damage was caused that the staff took weeks to clear up the resultant mess. The employees were so incensed that after pressure from them he withdrew further patronage to this body.

The grounds were the scene of many garden parties the largest event being the World Jamboree of the Scout Movement. Apparently it took the estate gardeners a few years to restore the turf on the great lawn to its original state after hundreds of tents had been pitched there for a week or so.

On the 13th July 1928 a Royal Air Force Bristol Bulldog Fighter crashed into Winter Hill in dense mist. The solitary occupant of this twin-seater plane, Flying Officer Walker having survived the impact, managed to make his way to Belmont Lodge, despite a broken arm and leg, to raise the alarm. When news broke the grounds were once again in the limelight and received much publicity.

John Magee was not a young man when he bought 'The Bungalow' and during his period of ownership there were no major alterations or additions made to the property. Following his death Thomas Magee was appointed executor of his estate and put 'The Bungalow' up for sale.

The Crown Hotel, Horwich – a Magee Marshall house. This was the terminus for trams carrying visitors to Lever Park.

Chapter 12 – Demolition

There was a widespread feeling that the property should be secured for the benefit of the people of the surrounding district. The idea was first mooted to Horwich Council by the clerk Mr. Jas Seddon and in January 1938 a meeting was held of representative local authorities – Horwich, Blackrod, Bolton, Adlington and Chorley Rural District Council. Representatives of Wigan and Aspull attended later meetings and on February 9th 1939, a letter was read from Mr. P. A. Barnes, secretary of the Council for the Preservation of Rural England who pledged support in the matter. Thomas Magee wrote to the Joint Committee expressing pleasure at their proposal to buy 'The Bungalow' and in spite of two other prospective buyers the Committee were offered first option to purchase for the price of £7,000.

The property was freehold but Liverpool Corporation had imposed a condition that 'The Bungalow' should not be used for any other purpose than that of a dwelling house. This restriction effectively stultified ideas for its development as a hotel or convalescent home which had been discussed.

With typical dilatoriness the Joint Committee appointed a sub-committee with three objectives, first to see if Thomas Magee would accept a lower offer, secondly to interview representatives of Liverpool Corporation regarding the imposed limitations on use of 'The Bungalow' and thirdly to prepare an estimate, as far as possible of the cost to maintain the property.

Before any replies were received Bolton Parks Committee informed Horwich Council that they were withdrawing from the negotiations and the decision was ratified by the Bolton Town Council at a meeting held on the 5th April 1939.

Despite requests to reconsider their decision on the grounds that this valuable amenity would be of most benefit to the people of Bolton, and the cost of upkeep only amounted to $\frac{1}{4}$d in the £ on the rates, Bolton Corporation chose not to reply.

Liverpool Corporation would not alter the conditions on use of 'The Bungalow' saying that it was a long established policy, firmly adhered to previously, of limiting the use of land in the neighbourhood of waterworks. It was regretted that no exception could be made in this case.

The outbreak of World War II meant that Local Authorities could not obtain a loan from the Ministry except for essential purposes, and buying 'The Bungalow' did not fall into this special category. A final appeal was made to Thomas Magee to defer the sale until such time as the Councils were in a

The Dovecote is minus its thatch and all the windows have been boarded up to prevent theft and damage.

It is difficult to imagine that this was once the beautifully furnished Morning Room.

The fixtures and fittings were of such superior quality that many were further utilised elsewhere after 'The Bungalow' was demolished.

The spiral staircase on the left led from the Winter Garden onto the flat roof of 'The Bungalow'. Picture taken during demolition 1948.

position to purchase the property but this was not possible, and so Liverpool Corporation succeeded in acquiring the property for the measley sum of £3,000.

During the war years 'The Bungalow' was used as a billet for troops. There was a dormitory in the ballroom and the movement of beds etc. resulted in many of the parquetry blocks being ripped up during this occupation and much wanton damage was caused generally.

The Barns incidentally were used for the storage of sugar and a series of 'nissen-huts' were erected on either side of the driveway leading to Rivington Hall, which was also used for storage purposes. (Harold Dickinson of Horwich was responsible for removing these huts after the war).

Accepting that much damage was caused to 'The Bungalow' during occupation by the armed forces it must also be remembered that John Magee had tenanted the place just prior to the outbreak of war. Therefore it could reasonably be argued that because the house was habitable before the army moved in, then the condition of the dwelling when the troops left was their responsibility and compensation was claimable for any damage from the Government. Whether any amount was paid or indeed ever claimed is not known but one thing is certain there was no money ever spent on repair work at 'The Bungalow'.

In May 1947 Liverpool Corporation announced its plans to demolish 'The Bungalow' stating that the building was a menance to the water supply in its present state and that renovation costs would be upwards of £20,000.

Dining Room – The broken window and damaged flooring give an idea of the extent of neglect.

Following an initial reaction of shocked indignation a number of stated 'resolute' intentions came to nothing – the road to Hell is paved with good intentions – so the demolition contractor was ordered to move in.

'The Bungalow' had been built to last and to lay the walls low was no easy task. The ballroom ceiling resisted even the explosives and there was finally no alternative but to sledge hammer it down.

Following demolition the grounds were plundered of many exotic shrubs and trees, sections of the lawn were rolled up and taken away and Nature began its own reclamation work.

The broken trellis work lying on the lawn border is from the Winter Garden running along the north front. (Photograph circa 1947).

Chapter 13 – The Bungalow Grounds – Present Day

The bungalow grounds are currently owned by the North West Water Authority which corporate body was formed in April 1974, following Local Government re-organisations. Since taking over from Liverpool Corporation there has been renewed interest in the once proud beauty of the place. In 1975 the Water Authority offered a grant of £2,500 when asking in the British Trust for Conservation Volunteers to clear the choked pathways, which had become almost impenetrable, and generally tidy the gardens for Public use. It was soon realised that the initial grant fell far short of the expenditure required and a further £7,000 was committed to cover work over a period terminating in March 1977.

Progress in reclamation and clearing of the grounds has been subject to the vicissitudes of the economic climate. High unemployment and constraints on Local Government spending have proved an advantage in that the ranks of volunteers have been swelled by those out of work wanting to utilise their time beneficially; whilst schemes sponsored by Central Government such as 'work experience' and 'youth opportunity' have led to supervised youngsters carrying out clearance projects.

It is extremely difficult to appreciate the scale of 'The Bungalow' because all that remains is an area of black and white tiles which were the flooring to lavatories situated near the entrance to the ballroom on the east side of the property. By following the arc created by the edge of the tiles it is possible to make out the circle which once contained the ballroom floor.

Whilst a number of the garden features remain virtually untouched there is no clue left to indicate the existence of others. Lever's Bridge and many of the paved walkways were ignored during demolition and have subsequently weathered well, but I was surprised to learn that a second pigeon tower, square in design with a four gabled roof once stood at the end of the pergola extending in front of 'The Bungalow' and the length of the pergolas proved another intriguing discovery.

The summerhouses are in a dilapidated state and extremely dirty internally after years of neglect although it is still possible to stand on the observation plateaux. The loggia (open sides gallery or arcade) below the pigeon tower are in a dangerous condition and notices are presently displayed warning people that they are unsafe. The Pigeon Tower has been fully renovated.

Weeds and shrubs have overgrown much of the great lawn but the square lawn, just below the bungalow site is still relatively flat. The orchestra steps remain and the stone base, which once supported the sun dial, is diagonally opposite.

Waterfalls, rocky pools and small lakes blend into the natural surroundings and the large 'Japanese' lake is an ever popular venue for visitors. It seems that there are no fish in this lake because it is either too cold or it could possibly be because of acidity from peat on the moors.

Schemes have been discussed to open up the area by improving the access roads which are currently so uneven that it is impossible to travel along them in a car; although they are negotiable by the 'Land Rover' type of vehicle. This idea would have an adverse effect in that it could well attract the commercial speculator and the wild, isolated appeal of the place would be lost. Fortunately this notion appears to have been 'shelved' for the time being at least because a locked metal barrier placed across the entrance from Sheep House Lane prevents unauthorised vehicular access. A similar barrier has been put across the entrance to the grounds where Belmont Lodge once stood.

Public Conveniences have been erected near the site of Bolton Lodge which were a much needed amenity. It is a pity that because of the activities of mindless vandals the toilets must be locked at certain times when unattended to prevent them being rendered unusable.

Attention has been focussed on the grounds in general and a great deal of improvement work has been carried out. Pathways have been cleared by cutting back the rhododendrons, fencing and walling has been repaired and sections of handrail constructed along the more precipitous stairways. The most untidy aspect of the gardens are the prolific rhododendron shrubs which, although beautiful in spring and early summer when adorned with multi-coloured blooms; provide an impenetrable barrier to many sections with their tangled branches. There is still a veritable jungle to work at and those pessimists who laughed at the idea of anything other than the native heather and bilberry growing there "should see them now".

Upkeep of the grounds is a costly ongoing commitment and great credit is due to the landowners and the various agencies responsible for financing and carrying out conservation work which is done for very little reward or appreciation in many cases. Without their activities we would lose much of our local heritage.

The recurring sentiment amongst those people to whom I have spoken was — "It is a shame that they ever pulled it down – it was a lovely place". 'The Bungalow' has gone forever but the grounds still provide the fascinating exercise of re-creating in the 'mind's eye' what shape and form these beautiful gardens once took.

Chapter Fourteen – Conclusion

It has been my purpose in the foregoing chapters to give a realistic impression of how 'Roynton Cottage' and 'The Bungalow' once looked. To describe and position, the garden features in the grounds and include reference to Lever Park have been secondary issues. Inevitably there are gaps in the story which it has proved impossible to fill because information was unavailable, but I feel sure that there is sufficient material included to facilitate the reader a reasonable level of understanding.

The story is an interesting one coloured with its share of incidents and the central characters include not one but two 'villains'. Edith Rigby who burned down 'Roynton Cottage' was the first, a courageous, if misguided, lady for whom it is difficult not to harbour a sneaking admiration. The second is Liverpool Corporation who took the decision to demolish 'The Bungalow' and robbed future generations of enjoying the 'gem' of the creation. It could also be argued that the Local Councils were 'guilty by default' in not pursuing more vigorously the purchase of this property for the price of £7,000, which would only serve as a deposit on a small terraced property these days.

It is of little consequence who was ultimately responsible for having 'The Bungalow' demolished and there is no point in an exercise to apportion blame because the fact is that the dwelling no longer exists and it is inconceivable that anyone would ever consider building a similar property there at any time in the future.

We are left with the grounds which are still beautiful even in an overgrown state and it cannot be denied that the lakes and waterfalls add enchantment to the place. The whole of this garden was a unique adventure in landscape design and the solution of those problems which it posed during construction will always evoke feelings of admiration for both the architects and builders alike who were responsible for such a successful creation.

Mr. Hitchen whose firm carried out the demolition removed a number of structures to a farm in Ellel, Galgate, Near Lancaster, where with permission from the present owner; these can still be seen. The dovecote from in front of 'The Bungalow' currently stands in the garden and although without its thatched covering is inhabited by doves. Garden shelters with their original wood lath seats have been rebuilt in the garden and the wrought iron screen from the musicians gallery is there although in a rusty state. Pergola columns plus some of the original beams and trellis work are there whilst a number of the doors from 'The Bungalow' have been incorporated into a house and barn a short distance from the farm.

With hindsight the time to purchase 'The Bungalow' was in 1939 from Thomas Magee and this plan failed principally because Bolton Corporation withdrew.

Whilst the last tenant of 'The Bungalow', John Magee, perpetuated the popularity of the residence by opening the grounds to the public and so on, the charm, legend and the special place it holds in people's affections must be attributed to Lord Lever. He has been variously described as a 'Captain of Industry' and a 'Genius' and whilst there is no argument with the former title the latter requires some comment.

Samuel Johnson (1709 – 1784) wrote that "The true genius is a mind of large general powers, accidentally determined to some particular direction". Cutting up the long bars of soap in his father's wholesale grocery business, 'accidentally' led Lord Lever to become the leading soap manufacturer of his time and there is ample evidence of his outstanding mental capabilities.

Aristotle (B.C. 384 – 322) said that "great geniuses are melancholy". Following the loss of his wife Lord Lever was a melancholy man internally and this loneliness was compounded by his almost total deafness.

Echoing Lord Lever's words on the death of his wife – 'without her influence there would have been neither a Port Sunlight, nor a Lever Brothers as we know it today', adds weight to the saying that behind every great man there is an equally great woman.

I shall always enjoy walking in the grounds and I know that this pleasurable pastime is enjoyed by many other people, particularly those who live locally and can visit there regularly. On Good Fridays Rivington will continue to host the thousands of visitors on their way to the Pike, many of whom will stay in the bungalow grounds and wander to their heart's content through this 'enigmatic' garden; whilst others press on to climb to the top of the Pike. The views from this vantage point are stunning but after savouring the conquering feeling for a short spell one realises that it is much colder there and the desire is to return back down the slopes for home.

Examining Lord Lever's decision to build his home on a mountain, I would be surprised if one man in a million would even contemplate such a project, let alone carry out the idea with such successful results. Rivington has been fortunate that a son of Bolton bore such an allegiance to the countryside where he rambled freely as a boy.

The mists of time will close over this chapter in our local history and dull the memory of 'The Bungalow' and grounds. If anyone in the future should ask about the origins and history of the mountain home of the soap millionaire it would please me that this work went some way towards providing an answer.

Bibliography

The following are major works to which I have referred:—

Lord Leverhulme	– The Second Viscount Leverhulme
Lord Leverhulme	– W. P. Jolly
About Rivington	– John Rawlinson
Heather In My Hat	– George Birtill
Anyon Kay's Horwich	– Brian Smith
Rivington	– Phoebe Hesketh
My Aunt Edith	– Phoebe Hesketh
A Short History of the Township of Rivington	– William Fergusson Irvine
The Life and Works of an English Landscape Artist	– Thomas H. Mawson
The Art and Craft of Garden making	– Thomas H. Mawson
Self Help	– Samuel Smiles
Baines History of Lancashire (Salford Hundred)	
The Building of the Beacon Tower on Rivington Pike	– Major G. N. Shawcross

List of Illustrations